IT'S NEVER THE SAME

IT'S NEVER THE SAME

A Priest's Struggle with Multiple Sclerosis

Fr Jimmy Doherty

VERITAS

First published 1988 by
Veritas Publications
7-8 Lower Abbey Street
Dublin 1

Copyright © Fr Jimmy Doherty 1988

ISBN 1 85390 087 7

Cover photography by Michael Gallagher
Cover design by Eddie McManus
Typesetting by Printset & Design Ltd, Dublin
Printed in the Republic of Ireland by
The Leinster Leader Ltd

Dedicated to the many unsung heroes and heroines
with multiple sclerosis

CONTENTS

ACKNOWLEDGEMENTS

A special word of thanks to Miss Mary Keogh, my housekeeper, receptionist and typist, not only for her patient typing of the manuscript but also for her caring and supportive presence.

My thanks to Rev. Fathers Brian Brady and Colm O'Doherty for their constructive reading of the drafts and their continuing friendship.

FOREWORD

This story, told with a simple and moving eloquence, is a story about the triumph of one man's mind, heart and spirit over the crippling illness, multiple sclerosis. It is a story which describes a young priest's journey through shock, suffering and despair into an unassailable understanding of the human condition.

Fr Jimmy Doherty's ministry has, from its beginning been characterised by a passionate, driving need to serve his community fully and faithfully — a need which is as robust and vigorous as ever today, despite the debilitating physical effects of MS. This book is an integral expression of his life of service: it offers a powerful message of hope, compassion and understanding not only to those who, in the words of Fr Jimmy 'are aware of death in the body', but to all of us living as we do in a broken, wounded world.

JOHN HUME, MP

ADSUM

On 18 June 1967 when I stood along with my class-mates in the main chapel of St Patrick's College, Maynooth, I knew my parents, family and some friends were present somewhere in the chapel, but my full attention was directed on the Archbishop of Dublin, Dr John Charles McQuaid, the celebrant of the ordination Eucharist.

As the roll-call began and each ordinand's name was called out in Latin, I waited, with some trepidation, to respond to my own name. *'Jacobus Doherty, Derriensis'* — *'Adsum'* — my response was spoken loudly and clearly and I stepped out to take my place in the sanctuary.

In the modern vernacular *'adsum'* is translated as 'I am present', yet I believe a fuller and more accurate translation is 'I am ready'.

After seven years' study, I suppose it could be said that a young man is ready or at least prepared intellectually to take on the role of priesthood. My theological training had been fairly extensive and intensive; my pastoral training had been sparse enough. I still remember with humour being shown how to pour water on a doll's head as Baptism training. While learning the intricate rubrical gestures and movements for celebrating Mass, I became quite adept at making quick cross-like movements over a wooden chalice.

The entire ordination ceremony moved along without a hitch. One could not expect the national Irish seminary to allow for any mistakes at such an important ceremony. So when I eventually moved out into the sunlight after the Mass, my first personal awareness of the fact that I was now a priest came home to me very forcibly when my own ageing bishop, Dr Neil Farren, and my parents knelt for my blessing.

People seemed to expect me to have been nervous, but my own inner happiness and joy were so strong that I did not seem to be aware of a nerve in my body. I was ready — or so I thought and believed.

The three-month delay before my appointment only caused me to become somewhat frustrated and annoyed. The starting-pistol had been fired, but for some reason or other the race had been postponed.

In October of that same year, I finally received my first appointment as curate to the parish of Glendermott, locally known as Waterside parish. Now I had an opportunity to put into practice what I had been prepared for and I suppose I could not have asked for a better training-ground.

Waterside parish was mainly urban with rural satellite communities. There were four churches, four hospitals, two secondary schools and five primary schools. It was a mixed community, with the Catholics in the minority, so challenges were present in abundance. And in my youthful exuberance, I responded to as many as I thought demanded attention. My day was busy, my weeks were crowded, my months were overloaded, my year was full and I enjoyed every minute of it.

As I spent my time in the parish, it soon became clear to me that Sunday was a focal point for the parish community.

Each Sunday, I watched hundreds of people coming to Masses. Somehow our working together each week climaxed in this unique form of prayer. I sensed a strange yet strong bond with my people as I walked out onto that altar. My preaching may have told them that God loved them; my telling them expressed my love for them. While it is not an easy task to face hundreds of people each Sunday and try to say something new and fresh to them, I loved that opportunity of being their priest.

I did not mind the long hours sitting in the confessional.

My first experience of nervousness came on the first day of hearing confessions. The schoolchildren had been marched down to the church. I waited in the sacristy to be joined by my fellow-priests at 11.00 a.m. At 10.50 a.m. I was walking up and down the sacristy, wringing my hands, quietly repeating the words of absolution over and over again. The buzz, chatter, giggles and noise of the several hundred children waiting in the church was like the first rumblings of an impending avalanche. A teacher gently knocked at the sacristy door and when I opened it, he must have seen a look of fear envelop my face. 'You may start now, if you wish, Father.'

'Yes', said I, 'I was just waiting for the other priests.' 'Sorry, Father, you're new and you're welcome to the parish.' We shook hands and I stepped out into the church to be met with about 600 staring young eyes and 300 suddenly tight mouths. And so began my professional priestly ministry.

As the months passed and my week began to take on some form of routine — daily Mass, weekend confessions, hospital, school and home visitation — I found myself being drawn to work with young people. This found expression in the local boys' club, situated in the basement of the parochial hall. The space was limited, the funds were low, the problems were many, but the morale was good. I decided to give a few nights each week to this particular ministry and I never regretted it, even though it ate into a lot of my own free time.

I had never fully realised how busy a priest's life could be, how demanding people could be, how high were others' expectations of me, how high my own expectations were, yet I seemed to thrive on hard work, on challenges and I found quite rapidly that I loved people and they reciprocated generously. As the months passed, I became more aware of my lack of readiness, but refused to be swamped by any sense of incompetence. If *adsum* meant 'I am ready', it meant for me a readiness to learn.

13

THE BEGINNINGS

The first year in priestly work was full, interesting and challenging. I marvelled at the inner strength of ordinary people who survived well despite many disadvantages... large families being able to live in cramped flats; men on the dole taking care of their children while their wives spent long arduous hours in shirt factories; men and women giving long hours to voluntary community work, helping others to cope with poverty, sickness and various tragic situations.

In the midst of all this I found men and women willing to give of their time and energy to work with the young boys in the club. One of our big tasks was to raise funds and plan for the future. As part of the fund-raising effort coupled with youth formation, we decided to stage a mini-pantomime, casted by club members and produced by the adults.

On one of the rehearsal nights, I went to the local primary school to prepare the classroom. A piano had to be moved into the rehearsal room. I was soon joined by one of the male helpers. He happened to be a male nurse in a psychiatric hospital. We began to move the piano. He pulled from one end while I pushed from the other. We had moved it a few feet when I suddenly collapsed onto the floor. The male nurse helped me onto a chair. Both of us were puzzled.

I still remember the conversation. 'What happened to you?' he asked. 'I don't know', I replied, 'I just lost power in my right leg and arm'.

'That's serious, Father. You should see about that.' Within two minutes, I felt power coming back into my limbs, stood up, and finished the job of positioning the piano. Looking back now, it was a very serious thing to happen. Yet the brevity of the attack along with the fact that I was able to resume activity so quickly somehow diminished the serious nature of it for me.

About two weeks later, when stepping into my car, turning on the ignition, adjusting to the proper gear, my right foot fell off the accelerator. Again within one minute, my foot felt normal and I drove without any difficulty. Foolishly I lived as if nothing had happened.

The following Saturday afternoon, I visited my parents at home. No-one made home-made soup like my mother. I was sitting at the table enjoying every mouthful when my right hand went limp, the spoon dropped onto the plate, and to this day I don't know why. I fell back off the chair onto the living-room floor. The panic lasted longer than the attack. Strong parental advice persuaded me to visit my doctor. He advised, and arranged for, a few days in hospital for tests. And so, where once I had been the regular visiting chaplain, I was now the patient. The tests were completed within three days.

The boys' club musical was to commence on the very night that I was released from hospital. Feeling as well as ever, I walked down to the club to help with preparations for the show.

An eerie silence descended on the club personnel when I walked through the door. This was explained to me most clearly the next day when I visited the local secondary school. When I entered the office of the headmistress, she turned a pale colour, her mouth dropped open and she stammered a hello.

I laughed and so did she after she told me that the school had just said a prayer for me that morning, fearing that death was imminent. Rumours had varied from a brain tumour to cancer and everything else that comes between them!

For the next two years, I had to visit the hospital clinic

every two months and report anything strange that I experienced in my body. I had a few things to report in that time — losing power of my right arm, experiencing double vision, and once the strange experience of my tongue refusing to do as I wanted. The difficulty with each and every attack was the extreme brevity of them. No attack lasted longer than forty-five seconds. The hospital visits continued, tests were ongoing but no particular result was forthcoming.

Then, just as quickly and suddenly as they had started, the attacks stopped completely. The hospital neurologist said that I need not return unless something particular happened. And just as I was leaving him on my last visit, he asked, 'You're sure that nothing is worrying you, Father?'

That question stayed with me for a few weeks. I was concerned about the club's fund-raising, there were several difficult marriage problems in which I was involved as counsellor, my father had not been keeping well — was I worrying too much about any of these?

But the activity of the parish caught me in its stream again and I began to give myself to the many and varied needs of parish life.

STRESS

I think back at times today to the amount of stress under which I was working in Waterside parish.

While I can say that I rarely felt fear, there were some particular stress-provoking situations which I faced along with my fellow-priests in the seventies. I do not believe that I was any more courageous than any priest or minister living in a situation in which death on the streets became quite commonplace. There is something about the human condition of the person that one learns to adapt to tension-filled moments. It has often been said that everyone remembers what he or she was doing on the day President John F. Kennedy was assassinated. It is equally true to say that every person in Derry City remembers what he or she was doing on Bloody Sunday in 1972. I had been physically present at almost every Civil Rights march that had taken place in Derry since 1968. In the early seventies, I had undertaken, with the help of teenagers, to run a Sunday afternoon programme for children under ten years of age. On Bloody Sunday, there had been a series of events arranged for the children in Waterside parish from 2 p.m. to 4 p.m. Many of the young teenagers went to the march in the city centre and I decided to forego the march in order to help supervise the children's activities. I was just leaving the club premises at 4.30 p.m. on that particular Sunday when I heard that there had been shooting at the march. Information about those events was clouded by many rumours and I found it hard to believe that people had been shot on the streets of Derry by the British army. The television news that evening confirmed that a number of people were dead. As I was on hospital duty that evening, I decided to go to Altnagelvin Hospital and give what assistance I could. My memory of the visit to the hospital morgue will remain with me for the rest of my life. Bodies were being brought in and laid on the ground surface of the morgue, each body being covered with a sheet. Not knowing who had or had not been anointed, I proceeded to anoint each body as it lay prone and stiff on the floor. It was an eerie experience as policemen and army personnel were in constant attention. For the next number of hours, I met relatives and friends who had come to identify bodies. Their constant screaming and crying penetrated my brain and my heart. I stayed at the hospital until midnight and eventually made my way back to the parochial house and went to bed as if in a daze. The numbness which I experienced was shot through with painful attacks of grief and anger. The emotion of anger was the one that caused me most problems. I can still remember walking up to St Mary's Church in Creggan for the funeral Mass of the victims and wondering would it not be best to join, and encourage others to join, the Irish Provisional Army.

But I know that these thoughts were issuing from anger within myself and if I were to give expression to such anger by revenge killing, that I would be turning my back on my basic belief in Jesus Christ and his message of love and he did ask us to include 'our enemies' in that love. I was also aware of the many young people within the youth club which I served and I felt a stronger desire to help them understand and try to live the Gospel message, rather than a message of hate and revenge. This attitude was put under further pressure when in 1973, a public house in Waterside parish was attacked by gunmen who sprayed it with machine-gun fire. Again I was on duty and when I reached the public house, an angry crowd was gathering outside. Once again I spent some time walking over dead bodies with blood splattered on the floor. This was the first extreme act of 'sectarianism' within our parish, but this time my innermost desire was to try to heal community division rather than seek revenge.

With the help of a very Christian Presbyterian minister, we established mixed adult and youth groupings. If we could learn to listen to one another, we might learn to love one another and love drives out fear. By sharing our different viewpoints and learning about each other's lifestyles, we might be able to destroy ignorance. Fear and ignorance were most certainly two evils which stalked our community.

These were the two most significant stressful events in my early priesthood. And yet almost once per month for several years, I found myself on the streets trying to calm angry teenagers and to separate warring factions. Another particular incident which stands out in my mind occurred one evening when a group of people came to the parochial house to inform me that a young Catholic man had been kidnapped by an extreme unionist force. I was standing listening to the allegations on Chapel Road just beside the parish church. At this time in our community, people had become very polarised and very definite nationalist and unionist ghettoes had been in existence for some time. The political and religious barriers were dovetailed in a very confusing and unhealthy manner. The Catholic men were talking angrily about moving into the Protestant estate where they believed the young man was being held. I could see the possibility of sectarian unrest unfolding before my eyes.

As we talked, argued and sought some resolution to the particular problem, a number of army jeeps approached us. I walked to the jeeps and asked to speak to the person in charge. I do not remember his rank but I suggested that they go to the unionist estate and make enquiries. I also volunteered to go with them. I asked my own people to do nothing but wait until I returned. They agreed.

It was the first time that I sat in an army jeep and as we travelled to the unionist ghetto, the army captain (if that was his rank) seemed to realise the delicacy of the operation. We arrived at the estate within ten minutes to see a line of masked men blocking off the entrance to the estate. The captain and I got out of the jeep and walked towards the line. Each masked man had a cudgel which he beat on the ground in perfect timing to the walk of the captain and myself. I felt a cold sweat break out on my back. When we reached the human barricade, I again asked to speak to the person in charge. One of the masked men stepped forward and in a broad Belfast accent he asked the nature of our visit. I simply said that if a Catholic man was being held hostage within the estate that it would be for the good of the whole community if he were released immediately. The masked man denied all knowledge of it. The army captain said that if there was no action within an hour that the army would come and make a thorough search of the estate. We then left to walk back to the jeeps with the cudgels beating out our walking pace on the ground.

I returned to my people and asked them to wait. The army left and I travelled up to the centre of the Catholic estate to try to maintain some calm. Many little groups of men were gathering and a foreboding silence seemed to descend on the estate as night fell. At that moment a brother of the kidnapped man approached me to say that he was going home to join his family in saying the rosary. I often ask myself even yet, should I not have gone and said my prayers? I simply walked back and forth through the streets and felt the strained stares of my own people.

After about fifteen minutes, someone ran up to me to say that the young kidnapped man had been found and he had been taken to a house within the estate. When I reached the house, he was being questioned by men who said they were seeking information for the IRA. The young man was sitting in a chair in a shocked state. His body had been burnt by cigarette ends. He said that he did not know where he had been held as he had been blindfolded but he had heard one of his captors saying, 'There's a bloody vicar and soldier

20

outside.' Shortly after that, he had been put into a car and dumped on a road adjacent to the Catholic ghetto. After arranging for him to have a strong cup of tea, I had him taken to his brother's home.

Then I just sat in my car and thanked God for his safe release. I seemed to be in a daze when someone came to my car to inform me that the IRA had kidnapped a Protestant man.

Once again I was pleading with men of extreme views to release their captive. I was promised that he would be released after one hour and no harm would come to him. I replied that I would not leave the area until this promise was kept. Just short of the hour, I saw the Protestant man walking to his car and driving off. As far as I could see, he was unharmed.

As I sat in my parochial house that night, I wondered about the whole messy situation. Something had to be done to ease community tension, to break down sectarian barriers, to put the Gospel message into practice. I was not a politician and did not want to be sucked into that way of being. But I was a priest and I believed in the message of Christ's Kingdom — aware that there was no short-cut that bypassed pain, suffering and crucifixion.

One of the saddest events in which I was involved occurred during the time when I was working with a group of Catholic and Protestant men. We had been meeting regularly in an effort to reach across the barriers which had divided us. As we grew in friendship and understanding there arose among us a desire to reach out to the young people in our community. After a lot of deliberation and detailed preparation, we chose thirty young boys, aged about fifteen years of age and took them to Corrymeela for a fortnight of adventure, sharing, listening and talking together.

The group was equally divided between Catholics and Protestants. There were about ten adults from our community acting as supervisors and twenty-two adults from various countries in Europe who came to participate in the venture. After the fortnight in Corrymeela, we had an eight-week programme drawn up so that when the young people returned, they could be encouraged to stay together and to work together.

The first night in Corrymeela was devastating as the boys refused to sleep in their rooms. It was our intention that a Protestant boy and a Catholic boy would share a room together. There was little sleep and a lot of supervision that first night. Things improved a little on the second night. As lights out approached on the third night, I found little groups of four or six boys in each bedroom chatting easily and pleading with me for an extra half-hour's conversation. The fortnight then passed very quickly and new friendships were born before our very eyes.

We eventually had to return home and the European visitors were to supervise the eight weeks of work. Gardens were to be dug in each other's ghettoes, youth clubs were to be refurbished, old-age pensioners' homes were to be papered and painted.

But within a fortnight of returning home, the group of thirty had been reduced to twelve. And after three weeks there were only two Catholic boys left.

The main reason for the drop-off in numbers was intimidation. Protestant boys were threatened by other Protestants and Catholic boys were threatened by other Catholics. The reality of the polarised ghettoes once more tore the dream to shreds. It became impossible to hope for true reconciliation if people refused to live together and as long as they held on to their prejudices, their fears and their ignorance.

Several years after this, I had a sense of real impotence, when several of those young boys who had been to Corrymeela ended up in prison because of sectarian violence. Any further work with young people of mixed faiths had to be done in secret. I persevered with this work for the rest of my time in Waterside parish but at times I felt as if I were trying to empty the Atlantic ocean using a bucket filled with holes. And I believe that many young men are in prison today for the sins of their adults. Somehow we have failed them.

The violence that still creates havoc on our streets may be traced to the bitterness, the hatred, the prejudice that resides in the hearts of many respectable adults.

It was a strange time for the priest to respond to his pastoral duties. The entire situation seemed to reflect what you might see on the cinema screen. Yet at the time it was my only real world. I'm sure every priest and minister has his own stories to tell, stories which would seem to fit into a comic-book.

Because of the way life seemed to be crazed, even the most normal action could take on a bizarre turn. As I sat in the parochial house in Waterside one night, I received a telephone call from a family in the Rosemount area of Derry, which is situated between what people now refer to as the Bogside and Creggan areas. The telephone call was actually from a mother who was anxious that I advise her about a particular family problem. The upshot of it was that I told the woman that I would come to visit her family that night.

Derry was particularly quiet as I travelled through it and the time was about 11 p.m. As I made my way up Creggan street heading towards Rosemount, I saw the familiar red light of a street check-point. I slowed to a stop, put down my window and reached for my driving licence. A soldier opened my car door, told me to step out with my driving licence in my hand and marched me to an adjacent police station. I was very conscious that no-one else was in sight and when we came to the police station, he advised that I lean on the wall with my arms to support me and to keep my legs wide apart. He reached over me, took my licence and called to another soldier who was told to check out my identity. I stood there in a rather uncomfortable posture. I could feel the rifle pressed against my back. I was held for about three or four minutes. It seemed much longer.

I heard a voice coming from the darkness, 'He's clear, let him go'. I was told to turn around, the licence was returned and I was asked to leave. By the time I got to the house of the woman who had telephoned, I was more glad of the tea than she was of my advice.

A few weeks later I received a message that a man from my own parish wished to see a priest: I just happened to be on call. His story reflected the strange things which were soon to become commonplace in our city. His car had been hijacked and he went in search of it. He eventually found it in one of the so-called 'no-go' areas. He got into his car and drove away. But he heard strange rattlings from the boot. He stopped to check and to his amazement, there were a number of rifles lying loosely together in his boot. He panicked and immediately drove to the local police station, gave his story and left his car for examination. However, on returning home, the IRA telephoned him and on hearing his story, told him to be at a certain spot at a definite time in the 'no-go' area. He was very frightened. Without thinking too much, I told him that I would take his place and see what I could do.

I travelled to the spot at the correct time, parked my car and stood and waited. Within minutes a car slowed at the kerbside and the masked faces were my obvious clue as to the identity of the occupants. I went to the car and said that I was representing the man whose car had been hijacked. I was told to get into the car, which I did, and we sped away. The driver then stopped at a particular street and said that he would have to make a phone call. Another man remained in the back of the car and kept watch over me with his rifle not far from my neck. I engaged him in some conversation and when I assured him that I was not going to run away, he relaxed his rifle. The conversation was rather strained and I think both of us were relieved when the driver returned to say that I could go and that no action was to be taken against the man whose car had been hijacked. As I drove home I asked myself what normal priestly duties were.

So my work increased as did my stress. Yet I was fit and strong and my days were not long enough for all that I wished to do.

Then came the rare sensation of pins and needles in my legs. These came and went during the day but returned more forcibly each night. And I began to feel more and more tired. I simply put this down to my work-load and I tried to cut back on some of that. I know now that I was not being fair to myself. I was trying to respond to every need as it arose and the only rest which I sought was my three weeks summer holidays. I talked myself into believing that I was suffering from burn-out. I tried to take an overall view of my life and knew in my heart that the centre of my priestly life had suffered, namely my prayer. 'To work is to pray,' was an old dictum that I had picked up along the way, and I had lost a source of inner peace and calm. So it became a priority for me to recapture the creative force of a priest's life, his personal relationship with Christ. With the help of a few other priests, we established a 'Fraternity' of priests, a group of men committed in friendship to support each other in ministry.

This commitment demanded a meeting each month and a resolve to enter into personal prayer. Such personal prayer was additional to the prayer of the breviary, daily Mass and the rosary.

This became one of the best decisions I have made since becoming a priest. Not only did I find good company, searching conversation and positive stimuli to prayer, but I discovered a very definite space in my priestly life and activity for relaxation and the human qualities of trust and friendship. The fraternity also provided a channel along which my own particular faith-quest could journey.

I am able now to look back and say that this was a very necessary and essential support for me as my body continued to weaken. During this time the pins and needles sensation never abated and the fatigue seemed to increase.

My father's death in the early seventies was the first major loss in my life and the first challenge to my faith. It was also the first event to bring tears to my eyes since I was a boy. I can now thank my father for that gift. It was something I had lacked. It is amazing how a busy lifestyle can numb a person to himself. I was reminded of what a thirteen-year-old girl had said to me after a club meeting one night, 'You are so busy being a busy priest that you are too busy'. And so I was. My involvement with organisations of varying descriptions, with so many different parish works and ministries, with other people's problems, had become so heavy that I had neglected giving time to myself. My own human development had been sacrificed for others' needs and crises.

When my new bishop, Dr Daly, changed me from my first parish after nine years and appointed me as his diocesan secretary, I was given the opportunity to reflect more deeply on my life and its priorities.

At first I thought that the intense pain which I experienced in my new post was merely the pain of loss, of being removed from a people whom I loved and by whom I was loved; then I thought it was just the lonely nature of being secretary. Some priests talked of it as being promotion, for me it was anything but. However, I was given the opportunity of looking more deeply at my relationship with God, my understanding of God, and my own self-worth and esteem. It became a painful period of growth.

GROWTH

Growing pains are often associated with young people whose bodies are becoming adult — but growth is a lifelong experience and the real pain of growth is the inner pain. My prayer life had begun to develop and my inner thought began to take on dimensions that I had never really known. I had learned a prayer of abandonment written by Fr Charles de Foucauld. The idea of abandonment to God is as difficult as it is beautiful. To be possessed by God rarely offers many sensible pleasures and so it is not sought after by the human person. And it is not that people do not want to love God — the difficulty is that he calls for *all* our hearts, *all* our souls, *all* our minds. I wanted to let go to God but I also knew that I wanted to hold on to some of myself. One is never more alone than when one is with God in prayer, I believe that this aloneness is something which only a believer knows about... the unbeliever does not worry him/herself with God or prayer. But I think of the times when I have sat in prayer and tried just to be with God. When I speak words of prayer or read the psalms, the words themselves seem to offer some form of tangible expression to my relationship with God. The pain rises when the words become mere words — what is the difference between reading words in a psalm and reading words in a dictionary? I believe in God, I believe him to be real but I am also aware of my own prayer, 'Help me when I find it hard to believe'. I know of moments when my awareness of God is so real that it is simply no problem to spend time with him; I know of other moments when I yearn for a tangible expression of the hidden God, even a tiny little light to give me encouragement, and it does not come. Then I wonder if I am only playing a game with God — if I could catch him, if I could hold him, he would scatter my darkness and make things easier for me. While it is comfortable to feel at home with God when I feel his closeness and gentleness, it is a great thing, even though more difficult, to be open to God and his mystery when I feel nothing in return. This was a time in my life when I experienced the pain of growing, the pain of learning to love and to give. This was a time when I wrote the following words:-

To fly and be at rest,
To move and be undisturbed,
To be and not to have,
To love and not possess.

It may be easy to conjecture that in some unknown and silent way I was being prepared to learn the meaning of weakness, the meaning of being dependent, of being out of control so that someone greater would be in control.

During all this time the pins and needles were constantly tingling in my arms and legs. But I had grown so accustomed to them that it was only at night as I lay on my bed that I was fully conscious of their presence. The fatigue persisted no matter what I did. I am still amazed that I did nothing about it — perhaps I was simply denying everything to myself. In some sense there was an aura of darkness that covered my whole life and I merely drifted from day to day.

As I sit now and think back to those times, I am quite amazed at my own personal attitude. It is said that many a priest suffers from the 'work-ethic', that he in some way proves his existence and worth by the amount of work which he undertakes. A deeply committed priest justifies his being by the hours of dedicated slogging which he can clock up. This also becomes his particular form of prayer — his prayer is expressed in his school-visitation, home-visitation, hours spent in marriage counselling, preparing couples for marriage and so on. And there is no doubt that a priest's days can be filled with such activity and if he is doing this work on behalf of God, then it becomes 'God-work' and this can be easily translated into prayer.

I can now see myself as having lived according to that ethic and while I also struggled to build a personal and intimate relationship with God in private prayer, yet my priesthood was at its fullest when I spent hours each day in the service of my people.

In some sense the attacks on my body were mere distractions from my work and at worst were frustrating moments in my fast living. My need to be busy and involved contributed a lot to my denial of sickness and my refusal to take it seriously. If I were to take it seriously, it might interfere with my priesthood.

AWARENESS

Then the bishop gave me a tremendous lift. He appointed me to be administrator of St Mary's, Creggan, which is a large city parish. It was a position that carried with it major responsibilities. I could not believe it to be true. And typical of me, I could not wait to get involved. I lived in a house with three curates, all of us sharing responsibility for a parish broken by unemployment, civil strife, inadequate housing conditions and yet filled with beautiful people.

I found it relatively easy to relate to the people from the first day of my appointment and I set about facing the many challenges that surrounded me. I loved it. This seemed to be just the thing which I needed. Until.... And there always seems to be an 'until'.... One morning I rose from bed and began washing. The lather was thick and plentiful. My arms and neck were washed thoroughly and then I covered my face with the lather. Suddenly my arms fell by my side and refused to move. I stumbled back to my bed trying to blow the soap-suds from my mouth and eyes and the only thing that I could do was to sit there. Within two minutes, power was restored to my arms and I washed the suds from my face, dried myself and stood looking at myself in the mirror. 'My God', I whispered, 'what is going wrong?'

A few weeks later as I finished Mass and was returning to the sacristy, my right leg began to drag. No one but I seemed to notice. It passed like all the little attacks and I said nothing to anyone. Weeks later again, while producing a play in the local Community Centre, I fell off the stage on to the rows of chairs. Everyone noticed. Gentle persuasion encouraged me to telephone my doctor and he told me to remain in the house until the consultant from the local hospital visited me. I was content to do that as I was preparing papers and talks for a retreat which I was to give to a group of seminary students in Cork.

The consultant was with me within two days. He carried out a few tests in my bedroom, checking reflexes in arms and legs and tickling my feet with a pencil.

When we returned to my study, he informed me that I was to be in hospital the following Monday for further tests. I protested as that was the first day of the seminary retreat. 'Surely', he said, 'those young men might care more for your health than you seem to'.

All protests were in vain. The retreat was cancelled and I was in hospital on Monday morning. The tests continued for two weeks — blood, urine, X-rays, brain-scan — all of which I submitted to with a nonchalance that must have annoyed the medical staff.

As no results were forthcoming and I was preparing to go home, the doctor then informed me that I had to go to the Royal Victoria Hospital, Belfast. I agreed, though rather reluctantly, as I had experienced no further attacks, although the sensation of pins and needles had moved up to my waist.

The doctors permitted me to arrange my own transport and one of my brothers duly drove me to Belfast. I left him in the hospital car-park, carried my little bag and proceeded to reception. The receptionist saw me coming and inquired about whom I was visiting. I still remember her quite shocked look when I informed her that I was to be a patient.

The four weeks which I spent there were long and hard. The tests were not particularly unpleasant, apart from the lumbar puncture, but the wondering and waiting weighed heavily upon me. There were about sixteen men in the same ward and as the days progressed, I discovered that about half of them had brain tumours or cancerous growths and some had only a few months to live. I remember saying to myself, almost for the first time, 'I am really sick'. And yet it was difficult to believe that as I felt so well.

I remember a particular damp Sunday afternoon. All my tests had been completed but no one came to tell me the results. It was a long, tiresome weekend.

As I sat looking out at the grounds becoming wetter and wetter, my spirits seemed to be in perfect harmony with the weather. Frightening thoughts passed through my mind — 'I have a tumour', 'I have six months to live', 'An operation would be pointless'. I sat at my little bedside table and began to write, the summary of which could have been put in a sentence — 'I want to live — I have a lot of love in me which I want to give'.

In a sense this was the first time I began to know of depression, like the heavy grey clouds that had settled over the hospital. On Monday morning the sister told me that the doctor would be in to see me. So I got on my best priestly face to hear the bad news. I braced myself and waited and when the young doctor said my sickness had no name, I felt disappointed, even cheated. It was compared to an electrical short in my system which caused the brain messages to be disrupted and I was assured that it would not cause me any serious damage. And so I was told I could go home.

Lying in bed for so long had left me feeling rather weak. So rather than returning immediately to the parish, I decided to spend a while at home with my mother. Each day, I went for a walk, extending it slightly each time, until within ten days, I was walking almost two miles daily and feeling fairly well. I was so glad to be able to return to the parish and although I did not feel a hundred per cent fit, I got back to my routine of duties.

There was a lot of work to be done and I set about it like an Olympic champion. After all, in my thinking, the 'Olympic-champion-priest' was the one who worked longest, worked hardest, and worked fastest. And now I had a slight handicap, like the jockey who had to carry a few extra weights. My vision was unimpaired, but my legs felt weak and the pins and needles persisted. But there were no external signs and so I tried to keep up a good image. Now I was torn within myself — still believing that if I slowed down my work rate the fatigue might get easier; yet still wanting to be the best priest that I could be for a people whom I loved dearly. It is easy for me now to say that my people would have been content with less. The difficulty in a sense was that I was not content with less. And this was further complicated with a growing question, 'What causes an electrical short in the system?'

DIAGNOSIS

The question about the cause of the illness burned within me. Fr Colm O'Doherty, a good friend with whom I have been blessed, suggested that I seek a second opinion. He recommended a neurologist in London whom I had known from work done previously with the Catholic Marriage Advisory Council. Fr Colm took responsibility for making contact and arranging an appointment. The date was fixed for Ash Wednesday 1981, so we flew to London. With not a little trepidation I sat in the neurologist's waiting room. He came and escorted me to a little room, tested my reflexes, looked at my eyes and had me carry out a few other minor little movements. It took about twenty minutes. In his office, he asked me had I not been told. I repeated for him the words which the young Belfast doctor had told me. He looked at me with calmness and firmness and asked, 'Do you want to know?' 'Yes, please,' I said. 'I want to know the cause, because I know my symptoms.' 'You have multiple sclerosis, albeit a benign form', he replied. I sat calmly listening to him as he explained what that meant, assuring me that the possibility of my being in a wheelchair was very remote — that he would write to my neurologist in Belfast.... His words faded away into nothingness, as my insides began to crumple. In my mind, I was screaming, 'Oh no, not me, not that, please God, no, no, no....' My screaming came from the awful frightening possibility of having to depend on a wheelchair for mobility.

It attacked in a most forceful way my work-ethic syndrome. After all, what worth would I have if I could not visit schools, visit homes, spend long hours counselling and helping people — what value would I have — this just could not be true. I suppose I had believed that my value was commensurate with the hours I spent at work. In civil life, people are paid according to productivity. I was caught into that same way of thinking — but sick people can be generally termed as 'invalids' and thereby have little to offer to the production scene. I know in my heart that this type of thinking is false but every profession, including priesthood, seemed to be tainted with it.

As we left the hospital, Fr Colm suggested that we get something to eat and asked what I would like to do. We looked at alternatives — join a group of priests for a quiet night of chatting and sharing or go out for the night. I looked at a newspaper and scanned the film advertisements. I knew I did not want to be in a group that night. Pointing to the paper, I said, 'Let's go to *Jazz Singer* — you'll really like Neil Diamond.' The film helped. I loved the singing. And yet within me, I felt a heavy deep cloud rising in my being as if it were ready to swamp me. My good friend gave me a lot of space, held back his questions and was willing to journey with me as befits a true companion. I dreaded going home and as I walked the few yards from the car to the door of my family home, I was trying to find words. My mother was in the sitting room with two of my sisters and a brother. I called my mother out to the back-kitchen, and as I tried to find words, I stuttered and just fell into her arms and the tears came — warm, gentle tears. I choked out into her ear, 'I have multiple sclerosis', and I can still feel her arms hugging me and hear her saying, 'You'll be all right . . . all right.' I was glad my mother was still alive to be able to hold me in a way that no other woman could — and yet I was sorry that, at her age, she had to know of that pain. It took me some time to unravel all the pain within me when I met my mother that evening. There were different levels of pain. In telling my mother of my sickness, I was admitting to the fact that in some way I was a failure. Secondly there was the terrible fear that she might blame herself along with my father for causing this disease within my body. Therefore my admitting to the illness might be taken as an accusation of both my parents and might be heard as a rejection of love. This tore me inside out because I loved my parents most dearly, yet by standing before my mother with a hidden and destroying virus in my body it might seem to her that I was placing her in the dock and pointing the finger of guilt at her. This disturbed me to my very roots. And that is why it was so important that my mother be alive, so sad that my father was dead, so rich that my mother and I could exchange embraces of love and gratitude. It became truly a life-saving moment. Such embraces are rare and most precious.

I returned to my parish and when I told my fellow curates of the diagnosis, they rallied round me in a very supportive way. It was at this time that I began to experience depression, even though I was not able to name it. 'Unless you deny yourself, take up your cross every day and follow me, you cannot be my disciple'. How often I had tried to pray that piece of scripture — now I was faced with the challenge of living it. 'Father not my will, but thine be done'. I asked myself, did I ever really mean that prayer. I cried to God in agony, 'I have given myself to you to share in your priesthood, have I been doing such a bad job, that you should do this to me?' Then I would get angry at myself for being angry with God. 'What road are you taking me on, Lord — where am I going?' And in the midst of all the pain, anger, and confusion, I was being brought to God in prayer in a way that I would never have realised. I suppose like most people I was running to God with my problem. Crises can force people into prayer, beseeching God to restore calm and peace. As my body reminded me every day that I was not well, I was going to God every day with my particular request. In a sense my sickness drove me daily to the God of my faith and by spending more time than usual with God in prayer, my relationship with him naturally developed. I wanted to be a priest — a broken one, yes — but a priest.

The next few months were full of turmoil, despair, depression, new beginnings, determination, weakness, courage. I can still remember with some anxiety a particular morning when I was shaving. Beside my shaving stick was a bottle of tablets which I had been given to offset any further double-vision attacks. I rolled the bottle between my thumb and finger and remember the thought that raced across my mind, 'one big swallow and it will be all over.' Then I smiled and placed the bottle back on the shelf. I did not know if I was serious — but the fact that the thought even came at all shocked me. Gradually I changed the routine of my work. No early morning Masses, only one Sunday Mass, no Baptisms, no night calls, and a few other minor changes. I also found at that time that I needed to rest each afternoon. I was surprised at myself being able to sleep each day from 2 p.m. until 4 p.m. Being administrator, there were certain duties that I was not able to delegate. The most burdensome one was the necessity to sit on the five school committees and I was chairperson of two of them. I can remember returning from a three-hour meeting of one such committee, driving back to the parochial house, going to my room, closing the door behind me and collapsing onto the floor, scattering the minutes sheets to the four corners of the room. As I lay there, I quietly but firmly prayed, 'Please, Lord, don't let the phone ring, because I just cannot respond to anything at this moment.' That was the loneliest moment of my priesthood and I cursed MS for it. My summer holidays could not come fast enough. I needed to get away. I needed to think. I needed to pray. My prayer was as broken as my body. God can heal it. God can inspire doctors to find a cure. My life is out of control. What next? And so I screamed and raged and suffered. I still have a note which I wrote at that time. 'I used to think that I had handed my life over to God — I know now that I hadn't. I had always held the reins and I didn't mind when God sat beside me — now he has taken the reins and I object. I feel I could be a better priest if I were in more control — maybe Creggan parish is too much....' I began my summer vacation with a big prayer, 'If God's strength revels in man's weakness, he should have terrific scope with me... if only I would trust him at the reins. I want to be his priest — the difficulty is being his priest on his terms'. Those were the words of my lips and my mind — but my heart shuddered at the thought of them. And yet how often I had prayed, 'Thy Kingdom come, thy will be done....' As the months passed by and my symptoms of pins and needles coupled with chronic fatigue persisted, I began to think seriously about my position as administrator of a parish with over ten thousand people.

I knew already that my fellow priests were more than willing to shoulder the burdens of the parish with me. In some sense it helped us as a group of four men. Because of my need for them to work with me, undertake some of my duties, the people in the parish began to talk of us as 'the team'. Yet still I suffered from the need to justify my life by my personal work rate and if it now became only a matter of delegating work to willing hands, I began to question the sort of priesthood which I exercised. My own personal pride demanded that I hold on to some power, some authority, some control. Within myself I was saying, 'I am not in a wheelchair yet and I'll fight it as long as I can'. No one was putting pressure on me to vacate my position and yet there was no one with whom I could share my dilemma, no one who could understand what was happening to me. The Dean of the diocese came to see me when I began to voice the possibility of my leaving. His kindness and warmth were more than welcome as he told me that I could handle the parish even in a wheelchair. But, he said, if the burden of work was seriously going to affect my health, then in fairness to myself, and for that reason alone, I should consider leaving. My ageing mother pleaded with me not to leave. 'You love the people, Jimmy,' she said, 'and they love you, you will not be happy if you leave'. Again the loneliness of my position became heightened and in July 1982, I made my final decision. My bishop accepted my resignation if that were my wish and he promised me a country curacy.

My mother still objected, believing it to be the wrong decision. A group of parishioners came to see me and asked me to consider staying on as a curate. I was deeply touched but knew how difficult it would be for someone to come in as administrator if I were still in the parish.

With my heart breaking into small fragments, I left Creggan parish in September 1982 and moved to the parish of Faughanvale. For the first time in my priesthood, I had a house of my own. One week after moving into the new house and meeting my new people, my mother died. I still do not know how I survived those months. The pain of bereavement was deep and acute and embraced the dying of my body, the loss of a people whom I loved dearly and the final letting go of my mother into death.

My mother had always been a strong woman, small but strong. She had given birth to nine children and we now had all grown into adulthood. She had suffered for the previous nine months with a heavy cold which had settled on her chest. The doctors diagnosed bronchitis and a late attack of asthma. We smiled together a lot as she tried to master an inhaler. She blew when she should have sucked and broke down laughing when she said, 'I just can't suck.' She too in her later years began to know of hospitals and tests. I had visited her on Saturday as usual but noticed quite a change in her appearance and suggested that the doctor be called again. When I returned to visit her on Sunday afternoon I suggested that all the family be told to come. I knew she was seriously ill. The doctor also came and she was quite disturbed at my mother's condition. My mother seemed to go into a heavy sleep, and apart from a brother in England and a sister in Scotland, the rest of the family were gathered around the bed. At about 4 p.m. my mother opened her eyes and looked at us and whispered gently, 'Goodbye, my beloved family.' and then went back to sleep again. I had to go out to my parish to celebrate evening Mass. Before I left, I spoke to my mother as she slept and told her I would hurry back.

Within one and a half hours, I had returned home to be met by my brother, Matt, who asked me to hurry. I ran upstairs and began anointing my mother again. She had already begun her final journey.

My tears mixed with the anointing oil, my words were choked, her breathing was slow. Her death was peaceful as she simply and gently stopped breathing.

Her death cut into me deeply as I collapsed in a heap onto the floor. Again it was some years later before I fully realised the grieving that swept over me — the grieving of three deaths, my mother's, my health, and my parish. The pain went deep and somehow in some strange way, the three grievings were not clearly separated or defined. That added to the darkness and confusion and erupted in an internal scream to God, 'What more do you want? Where are you taking me now? Why? Why? Oh why?'

The people of the new parish were more than kind and welcoming. Not knowing that I carried a debilitating sickness in my body, some few mused about why I did not get out more, move around the small estates. I gradually told them that I was not able to physically undertake particular projects. And while I was trying to settle and build up relationships with my people, I also felt within myself that I needed to get away, to think, to seek help. I applied for a three month priest renewal course and was released to do it. I was surprised at how well I was able to respond to the day's sessions and I found myself becoming actively involved in the searchings, sharings and open discussions.

During the eight-day directed retreat at the course, I had plenty of time to be alone with God. My question was still the same, 'What do you want of me? Where should I go?' One day as I lay in my room in silence, praying for God's guidance in my life, I had a most disturbing dream — yet it wasn't actually a dream, as I was fully conscious. In this dream, I found myself on a stage-coach, up front with the driver. There were six horses and Jesus Christ, the driver, had the reins. We were moving at a healthy speed down a dusty road. As I settled into the stage coach, he offered me three reins. We smiled, moved on and raised a lot of dust. Up ahead, I saw a T-junction and I said, 'Right, Jesus.' 'Left, Jimmy.' Then he took the reins from my hands and I was not able to resist and he turned left. I sat with arms folded and a frown on my face. As we progressed, I began to see the beauty of this new road, relaxed and smiled. At that moment he handed me back the three reins. Soon there was another T-junction. 'Left Jesus,' I said. 'Right, Jimmy.' 'No, left, Jesus.' The same procedure followed. He took my reins, turned right as I sat and huffed until I relaxed, smiled and received the reins again. Then I found myself praying deeply and with conviction. I prayed that at the next T-junction, I would say nothing, simply hand Jesus my three reins, allow him to take any turn which he desired and prayed, really prayed that if I did not like it, that he would hold on to me in case I fell off. I thought of the prayer of Fr Charles de Foucauld, 'I surrender myself into your hands, do with me what you will,' and wished I could really say it.

The 'dream' was clear, the message simple, yet the application of it all to my life was still confusing. It's only as I look back on the movements of my life that I have come to know that few of my decisions were made out of a clear head. I knew in my heart that I wanted to try to respond to Christ's guidance and allow him to control the reins. Yet I often wonder was it not I, myself, who actually made the decisions. While I had been only two years in my new parish of Faughanvale and had come to like the people a lot, my spirit was uneasy. Deep moods of depression swept over me from time to time — they touched on the pain of my mother's death, then again on the leaving of my previous parish, and then again on the dreaded disease of MS. It is quite easy to see now that I was totally confused. I am a bit surprised that no one else was able to reflect back to me some of my own confusion.

I negotiated once again with my bishop for a change of parish... and at these times my head was very much in control, but my heart was still in pieces. It was indeed a lonely place to be.

In September 1984, I was appointed as chaplain to Scoil Mhuire in Buncrana. Working with teenagers had never really worried me. The school job would leave me free of parochial duties which my body would find difficult and I prayed that God's will was being done. Again I had a house of my own and my housekeeper agreed to come with me. As I left for my new post, I remembered the words which I had spoken to my bishop, 'My body may be broken, but my heart and mind are still alive and well'. And it is easy for me to see now that this was a plea from a broken heart that I be not dismissed. And this came from my thinking that a priest's life can only be justified by his work level and if I could not do priestly activities, then maybe I would not be able to continue as a priest. I admit to this as more my problem than anyone else's and yet I also realise that I need to hear it being said back to me.

If a priest is a man who serves, then is he the better priest if he gives more service? Or indeed what is the real service that a priest has to offer? Can it be measured at all by activity?

THE TRUTH ABOUT MS

As I settled into my new home and began work within the school, I built up a routine for each day. The school did not make too many demands on me and I found I could meet most situations with a fair deal of competence and experience. I did not suffer any particular attacks but the fatigue persisted. I became somewhat involved with the local branch of the MS society and discovered I was being called upon to counsel and advise newly diagnosed sufferers of MS. Some of them had great difficulty in believing that I was a sufferer. I could still walk, move my hands, drive my car and there were absolutely no external signs of sickness. I was the healthiest looking 'invalid' in the country. I also became closely involved with an adult religious education course in Derry and loosely involved with a handicapped group also in Derry. I found that I was spending my days in Buncrana, and travelling to Derry at night for other activities. But deep inside, I was in knots. Emotionally this was expressed in outbursts of temper, of quietly shedding tears. During one of these periods I had a very touching experience. One afternoon as I sat in my room, ruminating about priesthood, missing the privilege and opportunity of saying Mass with a people, the tears filled my eyes and ran down my face. At that moment my housekeeper, Mary, entered, saw the state in which I was, knelt at my feet, looked up at my face and gently whispered, 'M ... S — Messy Stuff.'

I could do nothing but smile, and be grateful for her gentle company. These moments did not occur often but when they did come, my heart seemed to break wide open again and again. This was a side of me that few people saw. Again I cursed MS, but decided that I should enter the fight against it. Within a few months I put together in a little booklet some prayers, reflections and meditative words which I began to sell to raise funds for MS. I wrote the booklet, found a printer, published it and then set about distributing it. Within six weeks I had sold 7,000 copies.

I then called together a few priest friends with varied musical talents, put together a concert, rehearsed them, produced the show and staged it in three different centres. I involved some lay-people for comedy sketches, stage-men, and the orchestra. We packed three halls, received standing ovations and raised up to £6,000 for MS.

I thought it was going to kill me. I was acting MC and a front-curtain filler. During one of the shows when I was behind the wings changing into another outfit, I was unable to remove my shoes and trousers as I lost power in my lower limbs. The stage-crew facilitated the change of costume, stood me up on my feet and at the right cue, gave me a gentle push onto the stage. The audience probably thought that my wobbly entrance was part of the act. All in all, I found it great fun, not just performing in front of audiences but laughing and chatting during rehearsals.

My housekeeper, Mary, was also involved not only on stage but in preparing endless cups of tea at rehearsals. She was glad that I was laughing. And yet in some sense, I was defeating my own self. By being involved in so much activity, writing and distributing a book, producing and performing in a concert, I was giving support to the false notion that there was very little wrong with me. The physical fatigue and the emotional drain were not visible to anyone and I certainly was not revealing the fact that I suffered from a chronic and debilitating disease. I was happy to be engaged in activities that raised money for multiple sclerosis — but maybe somewhere within myself I was also feeding my own insatiable desire to work, trying to prove in some strange way that my personhood would be measured by the quantity of activity in which I was involved. I suppose there was a mixture of both motives and in the long run it got my adrenalin moving and brought a certain amount of success — not just financial success but personal success in that I was proving to myself that I would not be beaten. And at the same time, observers must have found it difficult to understand that I was in any way ill.

This creates a strange paradox — how do I look so healthy and yet carry within myself an incurable disease? Was I minimising the horror of the disease by appearing to manage so well? Each time I visited Derry, I would meet people who had once been my parishioners and without exception each would greet me with the same welcome, 'How are you Father you're looking great.'

I deliberately omit the punctuation marks in the typical question, because that is how it is addressed to me. Even if I replied 'terrible' to the statement/question, people would continue talking about how well I looked, not having heard my answer. Few people saw me dragging my leg, or stumbling along a corridor, or writhing in bed at night as if my spine were about to explode with a heat sensation. Many people have to sit in a wheelchair because they have lost power over their lower limbs, but they could still reflect a healthy face and body. This often becomes more the problem of the observer than the person with MS and it is something which I have personally had to deal with. Before I was afflicted with the disease, I was totally ignorant of its cause, nature, progression and prognosis. I had known a few persons who were in wheelchairs due to MS and I had assumed it was some sort of paralytic attack. I had never met a person with benign MS and never knew of its existence. So when I am faced with ignorance on the part of others, I am in no position to blame nor is there reason for blame. But there is cause for education, for removing the blind ignorance about the disease.

I attended a workshop run by Dr Elizabeth Kubler-Ross in 1986 and there learned more about my inner journey than

I had fully realised. She speaks of the five stages associated with the dying person, viz, denial, anger, bargaining, depression and finally acceptance. I discovered that these stages can be just as easily applied to an incurable illness, even though it does not hasten death. I also learned that a person can move from one stage to another, that there are no clear time boundaries and even if one has reached the stage of acceptance, one's mood may oscillate back into depression, anger or bargaining.

A death had taken place within my body. I had lost something most precious, namely, my health. I suppose I only came fully to appreciate good health when I had lost it. And as in a normal bereavement in the sense of the loss of a loved one, I had to work through this internal bereavement, shed my own tears, cry out either in anger or supplication to God, re-assess my own sense of worth and continue living.

Naturally this type of bereavement brings its own type of depression, a depression that is often aggravated by a sense of uselessness. This swept over me when I had to face the fact that I could not do the things I normally did. The loss of health brought with it other losses. I felt I had to relinquish my position as administrator of a large parish. In spite of assurances, there were moments when I felt as if I were a beggar, pleading for recognition, asking for my worth to be acknowledged. This cannot come easily mainly because so few people really understand what this 'Messy Stuff' does to a person. In this situation I have known how precious a friend is and I have a few close friends who offer me support which is essential. Often it might seem that I am accusing others for this pain and frustration in my life but I am simply sharing the turmoil that boils within me — a turmoil that prevented me from being able to be objective about myself and my lifestyle. I am saying that this is my journey, a confused one at that, and a journey with which I am slowly coming to terms. And when I acknowledge the preciousness of friends, it is simply that

I have found a few people who can hear my turmoil, who can sit by me when it seems to be overwhelming, who do not rush to find solutions or resolutions and who are big enough and brave enough to allow me to express my inner suffering. And it is also good for me to realise that I need others.

It is said that when a member of a family has a disease like cancer or alcoholism, then all the members of that family have to deal with the same disease. This only dawned on me gradually with regard to my own family and my disease. When my mother was alive, I used to spend my day off in her company. When she died, I made a very deliberate decision to make closer contact with my four brothers and four sisters and their families. I began to visit the family homes of those who still lived in Derry each Sunday afternoon and share their evening meal. I have been doing this consistently and regularly now for six years.

When I first told them of the nature of my disease, my sisters and sisters-in-law received the news with deep sadness and some tears. My brothers and brothers-in-law were stunned into silence. But all of them welcomed me with open arms into their homes and the strong family unit expressed itself in solidarity and support.

While we are a closely-knit family, serious personal conversation was never a commonplace event among us. Maybe like most Irish families, the women were more inclined to share their personal feelings than the men. My sisters often complained that I would not talk to them about myself and what the disease was like. I am more aware now that this was unfair to them. Like myself, they had little knowledge of multiple sclerosis and the only people with the disease whom they knew were crippled and in a wheelchair. They had been afraid that that was to be the course of the disease in me and so when I replied blandly 'I'm grand' to their question 'How are you?' I only helped to increase their inner anger and add to their anxiety.

And yet as I did not know if the disease was going to

progress, even though the doctors assured me it was benign, I can only think that I too was suppressing my own fears. Nor did I wish to load onto them my inner grumblings. Most of my energy was being directed at discovering a role for my ministry which would give me some sense of satisfaction and also would take cognisance of the disease. This caused me more anxiety and worry than the fact that I suffered from an incurable illness.

My brothers and sisters knew that my greatest problem was the symptom of exhaustion and they expressed their dismay and frustration when I told them of the many and varied projects in which I was involved. I just could not allow myself to do the minimum and simultaneously maximise my rest periods to the detriment of some creative energy force which I believe is a gift from God. My wild imagination seems to scream for expression and it drags my reluctant body along with it.

You can imagine the look of shock and disbelief, especially on the faces of my sisters, when I told them I was making a record. At this very moment of writing, my demo-tape has been sent to England to be made into records which I hope to sell to raise money for MS. A musician friend, Mr Philip Coyle, wrote the music for my lyrics. I titled the song, 'I am alive'. I played the tape for my family before I sent it off, and when they heard the following lyrics, it caused a few raised eyebrows.

Why do I cry,
Who hears my cry
In a world of much pain and broken people?
What's one small voice
Crying out on its own,
Can anybody hear,
Is anybody there,
Does anybody really care?
I am alive, I am alive, I am alive.
Yet how my world
Has fallen apart

By something in which I had no hand in.
And there was nothing that I could do,
No one seemed to know,
No one seemed to care,
Is anybody really there?
Does anybody really care?
I am alive, I am alive, I am alive.
This much I know,
The enemy's within
And while I fight
I will reach out
And witness for life and love.
I am alive, I am alive, I am alive.

I tried to express some of my own feelings of struggle and pain in the words of the song and while I did not intend to blame others in any way, one of my sisters asked, 'Do you really feel like that? Don't you know we care for you?'

I can recognise that it is more my inability to express such deep emotions and my consequent assumption that members of my family could not handle them that created the silent shell within which I was locked.

It was after this that a sister told me that when my mother had been told of my disease, she had wished it had been her rather than me. And while my brothers and sisters may share the same sentiment, I thank God that it was me and not one of them. I do not say this out of any martyr's wish or brave heart, but merely that I love my family so much that I would not wish anything so dreadful as MS on any of them.

Their support for me is expressed in an active interest in anything which I do. Our bond is cemented and reinforced as we gather once a year as a family to celebrate the Eucharist, usually at the anniversary of our parents' deaths.

On one such occasion we had gathered as usual, brothers, sisters, in-laws, nieces and nephews. The Mass was moving along gently and when we reached the part where a sign of peace is expressed, I paused to highlight it with a few words and inexplicably and surprisingly as I told them of my love for them, I burst into tears. I struggled through with Mass and after the final blessing, I rushed upstairs to remove my vestments and sat in my sister's bedroom. I felt so embarrassed. After about ten minutes, there came a knock on the door and two of my sisters entered to say there was a cup of tea ready. I tried to say I was sorry for the tears when one of them said, 'Jimmy, that was the most beautiful gift you ever gave our family. Now come down and have some tea'. I knew I had released something special among us all and as the night progressed, the fun increased and the only extra tears that night were tears of laughter.

I would also be aware of an extended family in my life. I have made some very particular friends from the parishes in which I have served. These families too welcome me with love and affection, none more so than the family of my housekeeper, Mary. Her parents, brothers and sister offer me another home which I respect and value. There are other significant individuals and families within this wider circle of friends and I am privileged to be held with great tenderness by them all.

This is a quality in life which many priests experience from their parish life. There are always particular people within a parish with which the priest makes a special connection. It can cause problems if a priest is seen to visit with a particular family more often than with others. He can then be accused of favouritism by other parishioners who feel ignored or slighted.

Yet I believe it to be a normal way of living. Just as families have particular friends with whom they socialise, so too the priest builds up similar types of relationships. There are homes wherein the priest can relax sufficiently to throw off his shoes, watch family television and even participate in family prayer. I believe a priest, like any human person, needs such familes and such human relationships. I have wondered when I observe my own married sisters and brothers, what it would have been like to be married. Over the years I have come to know families in which a spouse is afflicted with MS. I have been able to watch the warm and intimate care given by the healthy spouse, see the children hug and kiss their sick mother or father, feel the warm glow pervade the home. In my own life, as well as having the friendships of some very good men, I have also experienced the warmth and interest of women, both married and single. Women seem to ask questions with a tender caring nuance that few men do. And I wonder had I been married, would not the opportunities about speaking of myself intimately have abounded and would not the support which I needed in my blackest moments not been freely offered. I suppose I can only wonder about such 'what ifs'.

I also know of couples who have separated, and the source of their difficulty in marriage has been one or both's inability to cope with progressive debilitation due to MS. There still are significant women in my life who never forget my birthday or Christmas, who will make a point of telephoning me just to enquire how I am, who will visit me, even if it is only once a year and invite me out for a meal. But all such approaches are signs of the tender touch of the woman.

I remember when I was at college being told of a rule which was to guide a priest when driving his car. He was not supposed to be 'solus cum sola', that is, alone in his car with the only passenger being a woman in the front seat. At college we had received many sermons about 'particular friendships'. I can understand the thinking behind such cautionary guidelines, but I always felt that there were many times when they lacked some common sense. Two days after returning from college after my ordination, I was to visit a convent to celebrate Mass for the community. My mother had been invited as well. As she stepped into the car which I was driving, I smilingly reminded her of the 'solus cum sola' rule. 'I'm your mother and start driving,' she replied frostily. We both smiled and drove off. Yet some priests still have difficulty with this rule.

Rather than see all this as a problem for celibacy, I see it as being a challenge in intimacy. Because of their seminary training, priests were educated to shield themselves, to be defensive, to be awkwardly chauvinistic, to avoid any real contact with women. Having being reared in a family with four sisters who regularly had their friends in to tea or supper, and with four brothers who courted the friendship of women, I had found it relatively easy to be open and friendly with women.

I know there is an increasing number of priests today who leave the priesthood because of a significant woman who has entered their lives. Some of these men whom I know would gladly stay on in the Church as priests, but there is no space as yet for such people.

For myself, celibacy is part and parcel of the priesthood which I have accepted and try to live. Yet it does not mean that I do not relate to women. I have a beautiful memory of a family who have befriended me for many years. I visited the house one evening and bath-time had just begun. I settled myself on the sofa with the evening paper, listening to the laughter and giggles coming from the bathroom. There were four to be bathed and the parents were totally involved in the operation. As I sat and leafed through the paper, the door opened and a little girl came creeping over to me on all fours. She was about nine months old. The water was still dripping from her as she reached my legs, gingerly she reached a standing position and finally climbed onto my chest, where she laid her little head. Being the uncle of many little nieces and nephews, I was able to smile and cuddle her close. When her mother appeared with the large bath-towel, it was the signal for full-blown laughter. There are so many normal situations in which a priest will find himself which, to the narrow-minded, judgemental person, can appear risky and the priest can adopt the cold, distancing posture of the hardened celibate and thus do damage to his person and manhood and ultimately to his priesthood. If every woman is seen as a threat and a danger to the priest, then it is most likely that the problem lies with the priest who has failed to integrate his sexuality into life.

There is a risk in the whole field of intimacy — not just for the priest, but for every man and woman who explores that field. Yet if a celibate person hides behind strong defences, roles in life, positions and titles, then that person may kill the humanity with which he or she has been gifted by God. As people we are made to relate, to communicate, to be content and happy with ourselves and out of that sense of self-esteem and personal worth, to acknowledge the same qualities in others. I quote lines from a verse called 'Risking' by an unknown author:

— to laugh is to risk appearing the fool
— to weep is to risk appearing sentimental
— to reach out is to risk involvement
— to expose feelings is to risk exposing your true self
— to place your ideas and dreams before the crowd is to
  risk not being loved in return
— to live is to risk dying
— to hope is to risk despair
— to try is to risk failure

But the greatest hazard in life is to risk nothing.

The one who risks nothing does nothing and has nothing and finally is nothing. He may avoid suffering and sorrow, but he simply cannot learn, feel, change, grow or love. Chained by his certitude, he is a slave, he has forfeited freedom. Only one who risks is free.

But how is a celibate person really going to know if he or she would have made it in marriage? I am certainly aware of the fact that I do not have a relationship with a woman which allows for the openness and caring that we associate with a married couple. I would know of my own inner loneliness and miss the opportunity of children calling me 'Daddy,' rather than friends calling me 'Father'. And I have come to know of the deep pain of loneliness in my blackest moments. The intimate support of family would have been substantial at such times. Yet somewhere in my very being I know of my commitment to priesthood which encapsulates the whole notion of celibacy. It can be hard for any man or woman who is celibate to live through inner turmoil and pain. My own sense of aloneness is only heightened by my personal struggle with a very unusual disease.

This point was made more clear to me in 1987 when I was doing a radio interview. The interviewer, who happened to be a woman and maybe *because* she was a woman, spoke to me of the care that a sick spouse receives from the healthy spouse. She spoke of the warmth issuing from a close relationship and then asked what it was like for me in my relationship with the Church.

Certainly the official organisational Church looks after my housing accomodation and guarantees my security. Yet I wonder how much more difficult it would have been had I become incapacitated within a few months of ordination. Having worked as a priest in various parishes, I have many people whom I regard as friends, people with whom I can share much of my pain and anguish. When I meet parishioners whom I once served, I receive warm interest and support. It is from this 'church' that I get much-needed affirmation from individuals, both male and female, families, married couples and particular priests. In that context, I do not believe I am any different from the average Irish priest. I am sure it is not the same as the care that exists between a man and his wife; but so too I do not have the extra worry and responsibility for the upkeep of a house or the rearing of children. These cares must weigh heavily on a father and husband who finds himself called 'the Invalid.' I am not unhappy because I am not married, I believe that there is a special close relationship within marriage which is not mine; I am still willing to accept celibacy as it now stands but that does not mean that I avoid or pretend to ignore the warm intimacy and friendship of women with which I have been blessed. It is part of the sacrifice that is involved in being celibate.

I am blessed to share my life with a number of priest friends. I have already touched on the notion of 'fraternity'. This is a life-line for me. It is comprised of a group of six priests. We meet one day each month, chat together, have a meal together, pray together and celebrate Eucharist together. And if a man needs to talk about himself and a difficulty he may be experiencing, he is given five sets of listening ears. I remember one particular meeting day and I was feeling very low. As the group became aware of my condition, they encouraged me to speak... the only praying we did that day was to celebrate Eucharist; for the rest of the day, the group sat, listened and advised. No major resolutions were drawn up but I felt that I had been listened to and I was deeply grateful.

It is sometimes said that if you can holiday with someone, then you have found a friend. In July 1977 two priests from the fraternity and a teacher from Derry journeyed with me to a little Italian village called Spello, situated about ten miles from Assisi. We had read and studied together the writings of Carlo Carretto and, knowing that he spent six months each year at Spello, we had arranged to meet him there. He came to see us at a little hermitage, built on a hill outside Spello, which was to be the first of several encounters with Carlo, and the short, heavily-built appearance of the man in grey slacks, open-necked shirt, with a warm, accepting smile, who walked with the aid of a stick, belied the deep thought and richness of a man who lived with God. As he spoke about God, prayer, the Church and priesthood, the written words of his book began to spring to life again.

I uncovered a piece which I wrote in 1978 about our visit to Spello and on re-reading it I got a shiver down my spine about the condition of my life now. Allow me to quote from an essay which I wrote then:

Our hermitage was sparse and simple comprising three rooms; one in which we cooked and ate, one in which we slept, and one in which we prayed before a pyx placed in a triangular hole in the wall. The entire setting spoke loudly in its silence. There was no incense, no floral decoration, no prie-dieux, just a hole in the wall behind a bare altar surrounded by corded mats on which we sat or knelt. And a God-presence filled that emptiness. It seemed so far away from the churches to which we were accustomed. The Nazareth setting could not have been more real. As the hours passed by, thoughts of the priestly ministry flooded our minds. The priestly life is filled with so many meetings, so many official duties, that the time given directly to God in prayer is small. Yet here in this humble setting it seemed to be the only important thing to do — to give time to prayer. Can a priest give three hours of each day to prayer? Can poverty and simplicity return to the lifestyle of the modern priest? The stark nakedness of the host containing the God-life seemed to reveal even more clearly than before the closeness of God, the love of God.

There were moments in prayer during which we became more aware of our lives and what was happening to them. Many things tended to clutter up our lives. It was not only the burden of parish meetings but an unhealthy desire within oneself to seek success from the meetings; a sickly realisation that one's talks and even one's sermons were largely performances at which one wanted to impress, the anxiety we felt in the effort to please people and seek compliments for duties done; the burden of worrying about what people thought of one's work and person. As life took on a facade, so too did one's relationship with God. Somewhere along the way, life had become entangled. Carlo Carretto spoke of this as 'intoxication'. If we allow Christ to be the object of our prayer and our lives, then comes the gradual realisation that though involvement in the world may be as great as ever, it need never create anxiety in us. In time, our prayer can be a period during which we try to communicate with the God who is, the God of love, the God who knows all our concerns, the God who personally wants to meet us. The nakedness of poverty, simplicity, basic living, can help to remove all the idols that we sometimes substitute for God.

The physical work to which we were assigned at Spello still causes a bit of a laugh among our friends. Our task was to clear a field of stones by lifting them one by one, placing them in a bucket and then setting them out in piles. The pointlessness and futility of the work threatened to destroy us the first day. We were men who needed to see a definite purpose in actions, who felt happier when applying our minds to a problem — but lifting stones! But are actions which have a definite purpose the only meaningful actions for intelligent men? Can we be as simple and as poor as a piece of bread and a little wine in order to make Christ continually present among men? Maybe it is more true to say that God is afraid of anyone who tries to possess him; afraid of all our words and actions in prayer. The prayer which hands over everything to the Spirit and leaves us passive may be the form of prayer at which we should aim. No one can push God; demand an experience; search for a feeling — perseverance is more the key-note of the relationship. Our desire to succeed in prayer seems to come from a fear based on pride and self-sufficiency. And the trappings of a priest's life can become a threat because of their engulfing nature. So many things can possess us, our comforts, our organisations, our system, our clothes, our money, even our loved ones and, so possessed, our hearts are unable to be free enough to fly to God. The inner peace that results from freedom is to be treasured. Many priests struggle to dovetail their prayer with their activities believing that their best prayer will be found within their work. *Laborare est orare* has been a convenient excuse for men weighed down with parochial duties. And yet the time given to prayer is never wasted. Perhaps if priests gave actual hours to God in prayer, they would be a sign that they believe that God actually controls their lives and he will use their little rushing around for his own purposes. The priest is not the saviour of his parishioners — only the Lord saves; so why don't we let him?

That I am not able to pray is another favourite excuse... an excuse for running around doing God's work. Why not give him our uselessness and aridity? He might make much more of that than he would of our busyness. The priest is not really in control — he is a minister, a servant and the work of God does not stop with his feeble efforts and evangelising.

I am really no longer in control of my body, I can no longer decide what to do about certain things. My body dictates the boundaries of my activities. And I wonder, today, has God brought me to this 'place of uselessness' for his own purpose? Maybe I'd like to think so because it would be a 'God-reason' for being incapacitated. Or maybe, you, the reader, can answer that one.

LEARNING ABOUT SUFFERING

Having been a priest now for twenty years, I often think back to the words which I used to preach about suffering. My spine tingles even more with the thought of the many pious platitudes which I used.

The favourite priestly phrase is 'suffering unites a person more with the suffering Christ.' There is nothing wrong with that statement, the main difficulty being the fact that it is the concluding statement only after various premises have been lived through. To believe that it can stand on its own is to devalue the suffering of Christ and to avoid the suffering of the human individual. People will talk at length on the mystery of suffering rather than face into the mystery that is suffering. My own personal experience of suffering has changed my appreciation of it and my understanding of it.

There is much suffering in this world of ours that is directly attributable to man himself — but there is also a lot of suffering that is, or can be called 'innocent suffering.' When this is experienced, people begin to ask 'why' — it can be a why of confusion, or a why of wondering, or a why of utter pain. I too have asked those 'whys' and my questioning has led me to posit the statement that suffering as a mystery touches the mystery who is God.

It might seem rather simplistic or just delightfully vague to speak of 'mystery' as a well-known concept. I can say with some ease that Jesus Christ is God, but when I try to sit with this God either in prayer or thought, my mind feels closed and limited, I think of the many, many books which I have perused when studying the nature of God. I suppose they are man's efforts to try to place some tangible barriers around the God-figure, tangible boundaries which make some sense for the human mind. While having some, although necessarily limited understanding of God, I also know that my ignorance of God or about God is as infinite as God himself. It is within this context of thought that I try to use that phrase, 'the mystery that is suffering', just as there are many unanswered questions about God, so there are going to be many questions about suffering that have no answers.

Yet for me, mystery is not something which dismisses the human person, it is rather an invitation to grow, to search more deeply, to think more profoundly, to wonder more awesomely. When I try to apply my thinking to the mystery that is suffering, I come up with a few positive ideas. The mystery that is suffering, and here I am referring very specifically to the suffering of the innocent, people stricken with all types of diseases, the children born mentally and physically defective, the young mother cut down by a stroke and the many, many examples evident in human living.... This suffering is mysterious and yet speaks directly to our world today. And for me, it says in large bold print that the world is broken, the world has not got all the answers, the world is incomplete. These thoughts and ideas have issued from my own life experience in which suffering told me forcibly of my own brokenness. There is a temptation for healthy people, even governments and Church bodies, to try to sort out the world's problems by simply finding the right strategy. The raggedness of suffering challenges a philosophy that claims to have all the answers and in my opinion they cut through it so deeply that it reinforces my premise that the mystery that is suffering touches on the mystery who is God. There are some questions that just do not have clear-cut, razor-edged answers. God believes in us more than we believe in ourselves. When faced with insurmountable odds, the spirit of man responds with a strength and a force that is unbelievable or should I say, mysterious.

When I look back at my healthy years, I see a man moving from day to day with a fair amount of ease and comfort. I accepted responsibilities, made decisions and choices and carried the consequences. But when my body was broken, I had to face into deep moments of inner quiet and sometimes shocking periods of desperation to find a reason for living. My own dark and lonely moments touched places in my being that I never knew existed. I faced fear, disillusionment and loneliness that demanded I find new reasons for living. I had to learn to love myself all over again, brokenness included.

At least I was able to recognise this as a challenge and am still aware of my desire to meet it. I do not always succeed. Sometimes I discover within myself an anger that shakes me to my very bones. I can sit and curse MS and all its rottenness. I curse its permanence and the trail of havoc it leaves in its wake. I can scream at my all-loving God and then pray that I do not despair. I remember visiting a young lady who had reached the stage of needing a crutch while walking. I was amazed at her calm resignation and the simplicity with which she spoke of the probability of her needing a wheelchair within six months. Her calming smile and yet sure resolve to get on with living gave me hope in life. I suppose that gift of hope born out of real suffering is one person's gift to another. It was beautiful for me to see her rise above her own sickness and refuse to be beaten. I wonder about the many unsung heroes and heroines there are and how their presence to others is so valuable. I think at such moments of how Jesus Christ brought life out of death. I have come to appreciate in a deeper sense the humanity and loneliness of Jesus the person. When I have wandered into prayer, I have found myself beside Jesus in the garden of Gethsemane, understanding his perspiration becoming blood, knowing in a deeper way of his pain and loneliness on the Via Dolorosa and trying to stay with him as he uttered the prayer, 'Let this cup pass me by, yet not my will, but thine be done.'

Knowing this side of Jesus Christ, being able to get inside his skin and feel pain, confusion, loneliness, I find myself drawn to a God of real humanity. It is encouraging to know that my God had no neatly drawn boundaries, no pencilled horizons, no obvious paths with clearly marked signposts. I have been able to say to myself, 'It's all right to be lost, it's all right to be weak.' Slowly I have come to realise that being broken is an intimate part of my own humanity.

During this time in my own life I was searching out who this God is — when he grabs you, he seems to go for the legs, turns you upside down and confuses your direction. I have moved in my suffering from a passive belief in God, the Divinity, to a true personal belief in God who is Father.

I thought I had already made this journey, but it was only when I was faced with the blackness of doubt, the numbness of prayer, the powerlessness of my healing faith, that I came to believe in God in my nakedness. The book of Job became real reading for me, the suffering Christ became a real person for me, the eternal Father became my Father — not that the suffering was removed, but rather my attitude to it had changed, I did not like it any better, but from time to time I was able to say, 'If this is what God wants, then it's all right with me.'

DEPRESSION AND MS

As I write and think about the disease of multiple sclerosis, I find myself often using the word, 'depression'. In my counselling of other people with MS, they often refer to their experiences of depression.

I know that depression is not peculiar to MS; it is found in every walk of life and it is not necessarily linked to an incurable disease. Emotional difficulties, hard situations in life can create stress which in turn issues in depression. And there are chronic forms of depression with unknown or deep psychological causes. But I have known of depression arising from the effects of MS on my life.

At times it seems to come in waves and may or may not be related to a particular happening or situation. The whole day just seems to be black and a dark cloud hovers over my spirit. I mentioned in an earlier chapter that MS is a form of bereavement, and it has its own particular form of grief. Everybody knows something about bereavement in the normal sense of the word — the loss of a parent, or a spouse, or a child in death. It is a severe pain and only gradually do we learn to work our way through it and get on with living. Yet with bereavement, even after many years, there are moments which cause the pain to be resurrected, as for example, on the occasion of the anniversary or birthday of the deceased. On such occasions, a person can actually re-live the pain of loss, feel it cutting into the stomach, and tears can again fill the eyes.

With regard to an incurable illness, I have lost something very precious, namely my health. The loss in itself is bad enough but it has necessitated a change in my own lifestyle.

I had been the active priest, the man willing to work for long hours for the people whom I loved. I took pleasure in being able to provide people with services and it felt good to be needed for advice or help. In my new position as chaplain to a school, I can return to my house, do a little paper work or class preparation and then find myself with long hours of doing nothing. There are few telephone calls, irregular visits to my door and no urgent business on hand. From time to time when this mood would settle over me, I began to question my usefulness. Was I really needed? In what way was my priesthood being exercised? I found the schoolchildren good and playful; but schoolchildren are like a passing visitor. Within a few years, they pass through the school and disappear. This was different from the parish community which has a certain stability. By saying Mass with people regularly, I remembered how easily a relationship was built up between myself and my people. At church, people normally and usually sit in the same pews, and I felt a sense of belonging to them in a way that does not live within a school. At times I have talked of this to a few priests and tried to explain the sense of belonging which I had experienced within a parish set-up. People lived in streets and neighbourhoods and it was relatively easy to get to know them. As a priest I tried to visit the homes of my people and got a sense of the whole family — the parents' occupations, the children and their work or schools. I baptised the children, married some of the young men and women, and attended the funerals of the family. I was giving a service that was needed. In the school situation I found it difficult to remember the names of the students. When I might have managed to relate particular names to particular classes, the year was over and classes were changed. The older pupils left and a whole batch of first-years entered. At examination time, I would receive an influx of requests for prayers. A few times in the course of the year, students' parents may die and I would visit the home and meet a whole family. Every so often a young girl in the school might become pregnant and I may be called upon to advise and counsel. But the general run of things would be fairly routine.

Yet few of my priest-friends seemed to be able to appreciate this 'sense of belonging' about which I talked. Maybe had I more energy, I would have been able to create something similar within a school context. But for me at least, there was a sense of loneliness as chaplain which I had never experienced in a parish set-up.

I remember a particular time when I was suffering like this. I felt alone and lonely. It so happened that one of my priest-friends from the fraternity to which I belong rang me just to say 'hello'. He caught my mood over the telephone and when he realised I was in pain, he immediately said he was coming to visit me. Fr Brian Brady is his name and I doubt if he realised how much I appreciated his coming. For him it meant an hour's travel by car, a few hours' chat and company and then an hour's travel back to his home. Brian then took it upon himself to check with me from time to time and his visits became very important. I was also very frightened of how low I could become and my need to find resources within myself to offset states of low depression. I suppose I was still suffering from the idea that my worth was measured by my work-rate. Brian was one of the few people who could offer me affirmation without me feeling it was false.

It is easy to imagine how this feeling of depression can be heightened, when people jokingly speak to me of my bluffing. 'You're looking too well to be sick', is a common enough statement. I can understand this only too well — I knew nothing about MS until it hit my own body. I can even smile when I know that a person with a touch of influenza can look ten times worse than I do. In spite of my hidden internal viral enemy, I can look the healthiest man in the community. I know that generally I give no external signs to the casual observer. When my fatigue is so great that I am unable to attend some meeting, I simply telephone my apology and seek to be excused. Then I can become frustrated with other people's inability to comprehend or understand. Of course this frustration can also be put to good use — it has helped me to struggle through with this book in my desire to try to help people understand. I presume that the better informed people are about the nature of the illness, then the easier it will be for me to be truthful and honest. I have found myself frightened of taking my walking-stick in public in case I am faced with a barrage of new questions, 'Is it getting worse, Father?'. Maybe it is, but I also know of my need for some support if I am to be on my feet for some time.

I also know that it became important for me to be able to laugh more... not at people's ignorance, but just at the silly circumstances which sometimes arise.

I remember finishing Mass in the school for a young group and, as usual for me after Mass, I felt tired. Anyway I completed the necessary tidying up and then left the oratory to walk down the corridor. I must have been a bit wobbly in my walk because a twelve-year-old boy greeted me with a wide smile and the comment, 'Too much wine today, Father?' All I could do was return his smile and wobble on.

The depression can also be aggravated by the loneliness of the situation. What once I could do, I am now not able and no-one fully understands this except myself. I think I share that feeling with everyone to a greater or lesser degree. Everyone is in his or her own way discovering the challenges, difficulties and limitations of life and every person has to face that alone. Could it be that people who suffer from an incurable illness are better prepared to face the loneliest journey of all — death itself — and are able to do it out of a heightened appreciation of life and living?

In this whole area of depression, I write, naturally, as a lay person, with due deference to the medical profession.

The depression may cover my sadness, or anger, or guilt or even something that I am not fully aware of. There are times when I wish I could shed more tears than utter rough words of anger. I once spoke to a group of people with MS and I prefaced my remarks by saying that multiple sclerosis was a rotten disease. There was a spontaneous burst of laughter and I remember an elderly lady sitting in the front row in her wheelchair as she rocked back and forth and laughed heartily as she exclaimed, 'F... it, F... it,' I laughed with them all and nodded in agreement with the wheelchair lady. I thought it was one of the healthiest responses to my statement and one that could only be given by people who understood precisely what I was saying and knew instinctively that it was not pity or sympathy that I was seeking. The statement that MS is a rotten disease can stand on its own.

One of the unforeseen benefits of my sickness was the free time which I now had developed spontaneously. I found that people who were newly diagnosed as persons with MS would come to see me. I knew from my own experience that it can be a very difficult time. From my own training as a CMAC counsellor (Catholic Marriage Advisory Council), I had at least developed the skill of listening. I also knew about the underlying sadness or anger with which a person has to cope when faced with carrying an incurable illness.

While many people came to me and still come to me to know more about MS and what the future may hold for them, I listened to hear what emotional turmoil was going on underneath and then encouraged them in dealing with it. Most people who have been diagnosed as having MS are often content enough to hear me explaining in lay person's terms about the nature of the disease. I am able to give such people plenty of time, give little practical pieces of advice and recommend suitable reading material. A young woman sought me out about three months after being diagnosed. She was a teacher and she wondered whether she should resign from the post. I listened to her story for some time, saw that she was as mobile as I was and recommended that she discuss it with her headmaster.

Perhaps a few changes within the school system could safeguard her job, as for example a classroom on the ground floor, her free classes spread throughout the week, and a good healthy diet. I received a letter from her a year later in which she told me that she was more than adequately cared for and as a result she was happily continuing her occupation.

MS societies provide regular meetings for their members. Many of them are purely social to which wheelchair persons are transported. For some it is their only night out. In Donegal a self-help seminar is laid on each year in a hotel. This is a full weekend to which people with MS are invited. Doctors, social workers and physiotherapists are there to give talks and lead discussions. It is a very informative few days and a great social occasion. I usually attend as a participant and also offer Mass with all concerned. I believe these weekends help to give people a sense of their own dignity and self-worth.

FATIGUE

As I write this, 1987 is already drawing to a close. It may be interesting or helpful to state where I am now. While my pins and needles persist in my arms and legs, and occasionally I suffer from minor attacks of loss of power in my right leg, mainly due to excessive energy-loss by way of activity, my main symptom is one of fatigue. This too is a widely misunderstood condition.

Everyone gets tired, everyone knows what it is like to be out of breath, everyone knows the need to rest a little on a long walk — and that is the only measurement guide the healthy person has when told by a person with MS that he or she suffers from fatigue. Even to say that the fatigue is chronic does not make it any clearer.

I too remember what it was like to give myself physically to a football match and to come off the field perspiring and tired. I too remember the weakness I experienced after a six mile marathon; I too remember what it was like to stay up all night in a vigil service and to yawn my way into bed. Now I sleep for eight or nine hours each night and waken up tired. It takes my body about another hour to become alert. I may do a couple of hours work and then find I have to rest in a chair for an hour. If I go for a walk, my right leg begins to drag after a mile. If I celebrate Mass and there are a lot of people coming for Communion, I am able to stand distributing Communion for about ten minutes, but the walk back to the altar is wobbly and I am liable to stumble. After each Mass I have to sit down, not to get my breath back, but to allow my energy to be restored. This fatigue can be directly related to energy expended, but it is not always necessarily so. There are days when my body tells me it just wants to rest, that it is not able to function properly. I may receive a slight warning by the intensity of the pins and needles sensation in my legs or my whole body may feel so weak that I know I have to rest. And once again there are no external signs. I can look as healthy as anyone else as I sit on my chair.

This strange fatigue symptom was brought home to me very forcibly one night when I visited my home. I decided to take a warm, relaxing bath. My mother and sister had both gone to bed. I was lying back in the warmth of the water and feeling most calm and peaceful. Then I pulled out the plug and tried to get out of the bath. I found that I could not. I slipped and slithered, found that both arms and legs were useless; I did not want to cause panic at home. Somehow I managed to get the weight of my body over the side of the bath and just toppled on to the floor. I threw a towel over me and began pulling myself on my elbows from the bathroom into my bedroom. There I lay for a while on the floor and removed the excess water from my body. With some difficulty I got into my pyjamas and as I looked up at the height of the bed from my prone position on the floor, I imagined myself as Jack on the Beanstalk looking up at the giant's bed. With a lot of determination and not a little ingenuity, I made the climb, negotiated the bedclothes and lay back in wonder and disbelief. What would the morning bring?

I awoke next morning with all my faculties restored. Then I remembered reading in some book about the danger of hot baths for people with MS. From that day on, I showered. And so the fatigue persists, each day and every day. Sometimes it is worse than others and I am not always able to predict when it may be so. This causes some difficulty in planning my day's or week's schedule.

I may agree to give a two-day retreat or course one month from today, not knowing whether my body will be fit enough at the time. Fortunately, in the past six years I have had to cancel only two such engagements.

My only remedy is that of rest. If I take care of myself, avoid cluttering up my diary with varied appointments, I can get through most of my basic work. But there are times when I am not in full control of my diary.

Some of this comes from my perspective of priesthood and service. If people come to me for advice, help or consultation, I try to make myself available. But as every priest knows, one cannot dictate when people may need him. And if a number of urgent cases come within a space of a few hours, I'll still be available even though I may have to suffer for a time afterwards.

Fortunately I would regard myself as a fairly well organised type of person. And so when making appointments or arranging work duties, I also pencil in times of rest. In the long run I am the only person able to take care of myself. Having a prudent and caring housekeeper in Mary who also at times has to act as receptionist and secretary is a gift for which I am grateful.

Fatigue then is that particular element of MS that I have slowly had to learn to live with. It can cause frustration and disappointment when it actually interferes with particular plans which I would like to fulfil. But then I can be consoled within myself when I realise that I am not totally restricted and I have found that when I become involved in something which is of particular interest to me, my adrenalin seems to flow faster and the fatigue is quite bearable.

I suppose the best way to write of this is to say something now about my days, my months, my years. As I have already mentioned, I have quite a number of people who call on me for advice, help, support and counselling. This counselling and advice is not limited to people with MS. Many individuals and couples who are finding difficulties in life would call on me regularly seeking help. I would be one of the few priests who is not entangled in ordinary parish work or duties and so I find I have a most precious gift to offer them — time! I find in the average week that at least five individuals are visiting me. And when school closes in June my diary becomes filled with appointments of various kinds.

I am not really a man of hobbies. One of my pastimes would have been enjoying a game of snooker. My skill in that sport was fairly average at college but I found that I even had to give up that game. It is really amazing how much a second-rate amateur has to walk when playing a game of snooker. Unlike the professional who will sit for ten minutes while his opponent is clearing the table, amateurs of my class might pot a red ball, miss a colour, then my opponent might do the same and there is no real opportunity for sitting. If I play a game of snooker it can last from thirty to forty minutes and at the end of the game my right leg feels weak and wobbly.

I watch some television. I try to get the main news bulletins and I thoroughly enjoy an old black and white movie featuring stars like Spencer Tracy, James Cagney, Gary Cooper and especially James Stewart, whose slow drawl and laid-back style enthralls me. I secretly envy the character he portrayed.

I still read quite a lot and one of my favourite authors is Carlo Carretto. A few chapters of a book each night while lying in bed is a precious time in every day for me.

Over the years I have found I possess a rather unusual talent for a priest. I love producing concerts for stage. In 1985 I thought it might be a good idea if priests with particular musical talents would come together and perform on stage. There were already a number of 'holy shows' being performed in Ireland. I met with a number of priests whom I had invited to my home to discuss the idea of a stage production. I was happily surprised at their enthusiasm. All of them agreed to performing provided that the money would be given to MS charities. Their big fear was being asked by other needy and worthwhile charities to do more concerts and thereby opening themselves to a lot of travelling and allowing their time to be eaten away. The final decision was that they would do a limited number of shows for MS and if any further requests came in from other sources that I would take responsibility for refusing. I agreed.

I realised that I needed to call on all my organisational ability, not only for putting together a show, but also to ensure that I would take care of my rest periods.

I met with a good friend of mine who is also an excellent musician, Mr Philip Coyle, in January 1986. I outlined for him my format for the show and the different types of song that could be incorporated into it. The two main qualities of a variety show are, I believe, song and comedy. My housekeeper Mary Keogh, and a few friends, Mannix Doran, a young married couple, Carmel and Eugene Dunn, provided the personnel for the comedy sketches.

Philip Coyle and my eldest brother, Billy, who is also a drummer in a band, gathered together a number of men for the orchestra. I had also come to know a number of men who were an excellent stage crew and I asked them to help. Slowly but surely, a team of people were coming together. I heard somewhere that one of the major roles of the priest in society today is that of a talent-scout. This was a quality which I needed and which I exercised in this part of my life.

Anyway, after lots of rehearsals which were a mixture of good fun and much perspiration we were ready for the opening night. I experienced a new tingling feeling running up and down my spine as I waited behind the front curtain while the orchestra played the last remaining bars of their overture. And it is indeed a rare experience to be standing on a stage after a three-hour show and witness people leaping to their feet, whistling, cheering and applauding. One can collapse with a rare feeling of achievement.

Apart from being MC on the show, I was also on the stage with a group of priests who were performing Rock 'n Roll numbers from the sixties. The awful thing is that I cannot sing! One of my priest-friends, Brian Brady, said that I had a rare musical talent — he said I was one of the few people who could change key on the one note! But the sight of five priests singing Rock n' Roll numbers caused such wild enthusiasm among the audience that my voice did not seriously interfere with the good singing of the other priests.

I never realised how difficult it would be to phrase a letter of refusal to worthwhile charities. The news of the concert spread rapidly and I got requests from various parts of Ireland. It was particularly hard to say 'no' to some of my own class-mates from Maynooth.

The other difficulty was trying to explain to people why I would put myself through such arduous work at the risk of my own body. And I am aware that I am pushing my body to its limits. Yet I have such fun during the rehearsals and such a tremendous sense of achievement during the shows that it seems to perk up my whole system. And from a financial point of view it is very beneficial to MS societies.

The year following that first show, I received a surprise telephone call from BBC television. Tom O'Connor, a well-known singer and TV personality, was touring some cities in England and Northern Ireland and he was interested in featuring one of the groups from my show, viz. the Rock 'n Roll singing priests, in his show when he came to Derry. We just had the one song to perform. I contacted the other four priests involved and my musician friend and considering the fact that we already knew the song well and there would be no new material to learn, we agreed.

I still remember standing behind the stage scenery in the Guildhall in Derry with Fr Brian Brady, while the remaining priests were to enter from the other end. Suddenly silence seemed to descend on the auditorium. We waited for our cue. Neither of us wanted to peer out on stage as we were aware of the TV cameras. I found a little slit in the scenery and looked out to see the last few people leave the hall. We ran across the stage looking for the other priests but it was completely empty; there were not even any stage-crew, camera-men or sound-men. It was deserted. We ran out of the door behind the stage, down the back stairs where we met a security man. 'Get out', he said, 'we received a bombscare'. We ran out of the building, dressed in our Rock'n Roll gear, with the make up still damp on our faces. We felt slightly foolish standing outside on the street with the other artists and musicians. Rain had started to fall and passers-by were gently nudging each other and smiling. We all went to a local hotel to wait until the bomb was checked. We were not able to enter the Guildhall to find our proper clothes. Eventually the all-clear was given. Mr Tom O'Connor, as much a gentleman off the stage as on it, apologised for the mishap and everyone returned home.

Much to my surprise, a few weeks later, I received a telephone call to say that the Rock'n Roll clerics, with their musician, were invited to perform in the final television show of the year to be held in Liverpool. We were flown over, treated like mini-stars and we enjoyed the novelty and excitement of it all. As we waited in the green-room, dressed up again in our Rock'n Roll gear, Ian St John entered for a cup of coffee. Our minder introduced us to him as five priests. His stunned reaction revealed his obvious incredulity.

After the performance in front of a live audience and TV cameras, we returned to our dressing room to clean off the make up and don our clerical clothes. And just as we departed from the theatre to go back to the hotel, my right leg ceased to operate. Fr Brady and Philip Coyle physically supported me back to the hotel. After an hour's rest, I was able to resume the journey back to Ireland. People would regard my actions as foolish — to jeopardise my mobility for a song! Yet I got a lot of mileage in conversation and good fun out of the entire venture.

And in 1988, I was back producing another show. This time I persuaded twelve priests to join the group, plus my comedy team, faithful musicians and stage-crew. We performed in four halls and raised £9,600 for MS. It took me about four weeks to regain my lost energy and yet I know that I will probably do it again.

A lady telephoned me after one of the shows and said,

'You have done more for the priesthood than Bing Crosby in "Going My Way".' I took it as a very special compliment. But I must always take care and try to be prudent. One priest once said to me, 'Jimmy, you suffer from a terrible disease. All you have to do is to sit in your room, read books, watch television — you have to acknowledge your sickness.' Somehow, within myself, I feel that even if my disease progressed to the wheelchair stage, I'd still find it difficult to stay within my house.

Each year now for the past three or four years, I am asked to conduct youth retreats for young people aged between sixteen and nineteen. Any priest who has ever conducted a youth retreat knows the work that is involved. The preparation for a two-day retreat may take anything up to five or six weeks. Conducting such a retreat for around twenty-five enquiring, doubting, searching young minds is exhausting even for the healthiest of priests. I know it is not something I could physically do for long periods; yet I enjoy the challenge. After one such retreat conducted earlier this year for young men and women from a local school, several of them requested that they would like to continue meeting in my house on a regular basis. I agreed and was surprised on the first night that I was able to fit fifty-two young men and women into my sitting room. They continued to come to my house and with the help of the local curate, Fr Paul Frazer, my housekeeper, Mary, and Sister Helen Gallanagh, we tried to put some form of structure on the meetings. Central to the night's event was prayer and it is a very beautiful thing to have about fifty young people with an average age of eighteen coming to a priest's house to pray.

One particular retreat stands out clearly in my mind. A young sister of the Mercy order, Sr Nuala Doherty, and I had arranged to do a day's retreat with about twenty young boys and girls whose average age was fifteen. It is one of the most difficult age-groups with which to deal on a retreat. Religion is far from being their most popular subject. Sr

Nuala and I had prepared a programme which we thought might capture the imagination of the retreatants. The first hour was difficult and, during coffee break, Sr Nuala and I considered some contingency plans. As we entered the second session, one young man, Fergal McCrudden by name, began to seek answers for some big questions. Fergal chose the subject 'death' and began to delve deeper into its meaning. His questioning seemed to hold the attention of all. It also happened to be a subject that Sr Nuala and I had been discussing and reading about ourselves. Fergal, while interested in notions of heaven and the after-life, seemed more concerned about the nature of death itself. I can still hear him asking 'What's it like to die, Father?' 'Does a person know when he or she is going to die?', 'Is it like going to sleep?' We had little difficulty in filling the rest of the day. What happened afterwards made the whole discussion come alive. The retreat finished on Thursday evening when everyone went home. On Friday, Fergal played a football match for the school, went to a disco on Saturday night, Mass on Sunday and awakened on Monday morning feeling unwell. His mother told him to stay in bed and miss school while she did some shopping. When she returned from town she was told that Fergal was still unwell. She went to his bedroom and to her utter horror, discovered he was dead.

I attended the wakehouse that evening and could do little but shed tears. The entire family was crushed by the blow. The mother and I had some time together as she expressed thanks for the fact that Fergal had been on retreat. One of her comments to me still sounds strange. She told me that Fergal had not particularly liked the idea of going on retreat and yet when he returned he reported that he enjoyed it. He had made the unusual comment that all his questions were answered.

Meeting his class-mates was almost as difficult as meeting his family. The full reality of Fergal's questions had stunned them. It took several visits to the class to restore some calm and to enable them to work through their grieving.

I always feel when I conduct a retreat that the main work is done by God. The memory of that particular retreat confirms that idea for me. Fergal's questions had opened up many ideas with which I had been dealing in recent years. These ideas had been stimulated by Dr Elizabeth Kubler-Ross and I found myself reading many books on the subject. Grief counselling and grief therapy are very specialised techniques. I found that I wanted to learn more and more about them. Again because of the fact that my days are not highly structured I was being drawn into situations of families coping with cancer deaths.

While acknowledging my own inadequacies in this whole area, I also discovered that I was not totally out of my depth in dealing with particular death situations. And over the past few years, I have been privileged to journey with people who were facing death. It has made me more aware of my own mortality and enabled me to be more sensitive to people who are working through their own grief process. I appreciate more fully the way the Church in Ireland copes with the rituals of death. The open coffin, the wakehouse, the funeral Mass are all essential and healthy elements in helping people cope with death; and the Irish priest is part and parcel of this natural ritual.

My house is also used by a lay fraternity group from the parish, composed of five men and one woman. We meet regularly each month for scripture study, quiet prayer and sharing of the Eucharist.

Several years ago, I built a little 'poustinia', a house of retreat and prayer, on a hillside in county Derry. I visit this little house from time to time for some quiet peace and at times the local people would gather with me for prayer and Mass. And there is one significant little 'happening' which takes place in this house each Christmas night. Christmas day itself can become a very tiring day, feasting ourselves on turkey, ham and sweets and then curling up sleepily before a warm fire to watch television. Fr Colm O'Doherty and myself decided to go to the little house, named

'Nuabheatha', on Christmas night from 11 p.m. to midnight. Now each Christmas night we are joined there by about fifty or sixty people and we hold a carol service. So in spite of my physical disability, I have been brought into the lives of many groups and individuals. Pope John Paul II spoke of the need for evangelisation of peoples with particular emphasis on varied groupings. This has happened to me in my life without any deliberate planning and it seems to have become a type of special ministry within the Church structures and yet remains unstructured.

These types of events and gatherings continue to give me life and they have become expressions of my priesting. Someone nicknamed me Fr Freelance. That idea could be pushed a little far, but it does fit my lifestyle sometimes. Apart from all these things, I try to give some service to the parish in which I live. Now I say a Mass each Sunday for the people of Buncrana and that too is enlivening for me. If I become ill for whatever reason, none of these groupings suffer. Each has a life of its own. In fact just as I write, I am suffering from a strange sensation of numbness on the right side of my face. The doctor has prescribed a small course of steroids to try to ease whatever inflammation of the nervous system that may have occurred. It has already awakened in me the fear that the disease may be becoming slightly more aggravated. And yet there has been no change in my physical appearance. I ask myself if I have contributed to a worsening in my condition by my present work-rate. However, I do not want MS to dictate the boundaries of my living... as I said in my record 'I am alive'. While I am thinking that this numbness on my face is another attack and will probably and hopefully pass, it is an extra reminder that my body is sick. I suppose over the years I have adjusted to the constant presence of pins and needles and the horrible fatigue that is with me each day, but when a new symptom occurs I am forced to ponder and wonder just what is going on inside my body. At least this time I was able to speak to my family about it and their gentle support has been encouraging. Each day two or three of my brothers or sisters telephone to enquire about me. Yet there is no apparent sign for anyone to notice that things are just a little bit more difficult. And I find myself happy enough about that. People are very good but I dread the image of martyr. I am in touch at this very moment with particular people for whom life is rapidly drawing to a close. Their families are experiencing deep and acute pain.

The pain of people who love the sick person can be heavy and disturbing. The strong undercurrent is expressed in the phrase, 'I can really do nothing to alleviate your discomfort'. Yet their warm understanding presence is as supportive as the tablets that have to be swallowed each day. It is amazing how important a friend's visit is to me. That he or she would give me some of his/her time just to sit, chat and share a cup of tea is a gift that I have come to appreciate.

Initially I began this chapter to speak of fatigue as one of the major symptoms of MS; but I hear myself saying and I believe it to be right, that this one symptom, difficult as it may be, cannot and should not be allowed to dictate the quality of my life. Yes, it may impede, affect, limit certain activities and certainly change the lifestyle of a person, but the person is always bigger. I have come to understand better how and why a disabled person constructs a new way of living for himself/herself. Sometimes I feel more sorry for the healthy person who might be inclined to judge the handicapped by a productivity scale. And I just wish that people would not allow the handicapped person to feel dependent, either financially or emotionally. We are all part of society; some may be productive, adept at business, creating wealth and employment — that is their role and their gift to the community; others may be bringing more expensive gifts to the same community by their courage and bravery in the face of cruel odds. I remember attending the Worldwide International Conference on MS in Washington, USA, in 1987; an Australian gentleman who worked for an active MS branch spoke at a small gathering and said that every MS person should be given an honorary degree in medical science. All of us can acknowledge courage when we see it — there are thousands of people in Ireland with MS and their gifts to society are rarely noticed. The same principle applies to every sick and diseased person who manages to get through another day.

MY BELIEF AND UNBELIEF

Having been a Catholic priest now for twenty years, I am the sort of man who enjoys reading.

I read fewer novels now than I used to in my earlier priesthood and the books to which I am attracted would be within the realm of spiritual or philosophical works. I am a man who seems to need intellectual thought, wider spiritual horizons and to grope with questions that face all people in general. As a Catholic priest, I belong and am committed to the Roman Catholic Church. I find it quite a beautiful society to belong to and I see it as my wider or extended family. And like any family, there are occasions when tension and pain are part of the living experience. Sometimes the rules and discipline of my Church grate on me and on my freedom, yet it is within this family of faith that I discover and meet my God — in the light-wafered Eucharist, in the pain-searching joyful confession of my sinfulness, in the common faith-filled prayer of my fellow believers. So I am further challenged to live with the tension of the Church's discipline alongside the freedom given by God in faith. I know I am not big enough to step outside this faith-conscious group and reach out for God on my own. I am happy with my broken and wounded Church, because I know what it is like to be broken and wounded. It is true to say that I still meet doubts, mists and confusion. I never waken up any day and say 'Now I know it all, now I can see clearly.' More often than not I hear my own inner rumblings and questions as I try to reach out to the God of my life.

My first meeting with God was with the person of Jesus

Christ — he was the one person of the Godhead that I could read about, look at his life, hear his words — there were books written about him by people who touched him, walked with him, ate with him. The Gospels became precious insights into the God of my faith. In the Gospels, he reveals himself to me as a young God, an energetic God, an athletic God — a God young enough to jump over the barriers built by men — barriers of prejudice, narrow-mindedness, poverty, power, greed — a God who smashed his way through the silly man-made restrictions and laws. He is a God who allowed his body to be beaten, broken, crucified and rise triumphant. He faced man's great enemy, death, and conquered it. Yet in all of that, he knew of confusion, agony, frustration, isolation, loneliness, depression and he conquered them — not by avoiding or minimising them, but by living through them, taking them on board and feeling them in the depths of his own manhood.

I say this because I know that people in their own agony and pain can turn on God, blame him, accuse him and even reject him.

In my own relating to God, I found myself becoming angry with him, blaming him for allowing disease in my body and yet in spite of all this, my awareness of God became deeper and I never ended up by rejecting him. And I believe this is more his work and gift than my own resolution of the dilemma.

I believe in God, a God of love revealed to us in Jesus Christ because I believe in the wind that can blow away the drabness of our day, because I believe in the warmth of the sun that can bring a smile to my face, because I believe in the beauty of the rainbow that touches the sky with a vista of colour, because I believe in the touch of a hand that can make me feel wanted, because I believe in the encouraging smile and warm embrace that can make me feel loved, because I believe in the all-embracing forgiveness given to me freely by people I hurt, because I believe in the gurgling, giggling baby who just wants to be lifted and cuddled, because I believe in men and women who do not content themselves with things as they are but rather look to what they can become, because I believe in youth who see the future as theirs and want it better than the past, I believe in God because I believe, I hope, I love. And by the vision of life with which I have been blessed by multiple sclerosis, it enables me to look out on a world that is in itself already broken and fragmented. Woundedness and brokenness are not limited to bodily and physical functions. And maybe those of us who carry around broken bodies can speak loudly to the so-called healthy people of the world and remind them of their own inner brokenness. Life is not like sailing across a green lagoon under a heavenly blue sky being accompanied by the pleasant chirping of little birds; life knows of stress, pain, discomfort in all its aspects. There are few people in the world who do not know of trauma and tension — from the little child whose pet canary has died, or the young couple who suddenly have to face stringent financial difficulties due to unemployment, or the mother of three children who has been diagnosed as having cancer. On the wider scale there is the continual tension in all parts of the world caused by political friction and uneasy relationships, beginning with my own country in Northern Ireland, to the Gulf War, to the Ethiopian or Mozambique famines, to the constant threat of nuclear war. Everywhere and at all times we seem to live in a world of stress and confusion.

It was while thinking of this that I once wrote a prayer, which I entitled 'Man's Prayer.'

> And so I pray.
> I pray for the broken world,
> For a world that at last
> Has put God in a safe place;
> No longer does it try to kill him,
> That has failed.
> No longer does it treat him with indifference,

That has failed.
But it acknowledges him
As being on the periphery
And unknowingly has created its own
    emptiness and brokenness.
We pray for the governments of the world
Who try to go it alone,
Working out their insipid strategies.
We pray for a people
Who have become their own source of power.
We pray for ourselves
For failing to recognise the source of
    our incompleteness.
Who have finally marginalised God.
No wonder we have a sense of incompleteness.
Today in this empty and drifting century
We pray that we may give God his
    real place in the centre,
To fill our emptiness,
To be the source of our real power,
To enable us to love,
To enable us to be complete,
To be fully human
Made in his image and likeness.
We pray for the humility
of recognising who we are
And who God is.
We pray again to be able to pray,
We pray again to be able to love.

The sickness that man experiences in his own body and
spirit is in a sense a modern day prophecy. It speaks loudly
to the world that man is incomplete, that man does not have
all the answers. Sickness in the world is a constant reminder
that the world does not have all the answers. And I believe
that man is chasing after rainbows if he believes that by dint
of intellect, perseverance, employment of the right strategy,
that he will find all the answers to the questions which

disturb the modern mind. It is a more honest security to be able to live with one's own insecurities. And for a believer it is a steady bulwark to his faith to be open to a God of mystery, a God of surprises who allows the rain to fall on the just and unjust alike. Suffering and sickness which bear their own pain and bring their own questions do not negate man's inner being or spirit.

To quote a popular song written by another native Derry man, 'Man's spirit is bruised but never broken.' Indeed it is a gift of grace to bow before the God of life and death, the God of sickness and health, the God of the known and unknown, but I claim that even for the unbeliever, he can come to realise the insipidity of man's search for solutions. Man may be able to control great forces of power, may be able to blow our universe into annihilation, may be able by means of technological advancement to bring test-tube babies to life and yet in spite of all his intellectual powers, man cannot create a blade of grass out of nothing.

The sick and the ill may need the help and assistance of the able bodied and it is to their credit that they have come to that realisation; the sadness lies in the simple fact that the so-called healthy people are not aware of their need for the sick, the wounded and the broken. This psychological fact probably stems from the fact that man believes himself to be whole, believes himself to have things under control and therefore is not aware of his own inner vacuum, his own inner brokenness, his own inner incompleteness. In a very broad sense, it could be said that modern man is unable to make an act of faith, is unable to acknowledge a power greater than himself. In a way it could be said, speaking metaphorically, that modern man is an alcoholic but denies it. His thirst for greed, power, control have made him drunk.

My body is broken, my health is impaired and because of this I can doubt the existence of God or question his nature. At the same time, I can also recognise my inner need for God, my dependence on him and my love for him. I believe my act of faith in a caring God has more genuineness within it when it is spoken out of darkness, or numbness, or blackness, than when I speak it in comfort and security. But this has been, and still is, a painful journey. It would have been nice for me had my pastures remained forever green but somehow I believe that my faith in God now is richer even though it is disturbed by doubts, questionings and queries.

Not wishing to be in any way sacrilegious, I know a little more of Jesus' cry, 'My God, my God, why have you forsaken me?' And so my prayer can continue, 'I believe, yet help my unbelief.' I cannot hope to place neat boundaries around the God who is — if I could, he would cease to be God.

Nor am I any less a person because of my sickness, for surely it is part and parcel of being human to be broken and incomplete.

ADSUM

In the very first chapter of this book, I referred to the word which the young ordinand says on the day of his ordination to priesthood. I translated the word *adsum* as meaning 'I am ready.' In many ways it has taken me the best part of twenty years to be able to put meaning into that word. This is in no way to cast any aspersions on other priests — I am sure that they, like myself, meant that they were willing to be ready, willing to face both the known and unknown, challenges, difficulties, choices which evolved before them in priesthood.

Due to the affliction of my suffering and sickness, while living through its agony, frustration and pain, I am now able to say that new windows have been opened up for me as a person and as a priest.

I know myself to be more at ease with the chronically sick or the terminally ill. When in their presence, there is something more than sympathy, there is a mutual awareness of death in the body which can give rise to open and frank communication, there is real empathy. In such circumstances I have been blessed by the forthright exchange of thoughts, feelings, pain and joy. I'm not saying that every priest and counsellor has to suffer a personal disease for this to happen — just that I know myself to be more comfortable in such situations than I was fifteen years ago. My own self-assurance and ability to enter such areas has been heightened and strengthened because of my own brokenness.

I cannot count the number of people who have come to me seeking advice or merely to share their own experience shortly after they have been diagnosed as having multiple sclerosis. Both they and I are grateful for such meetings.

I have come to a fuller appreciation of the gift of health since I lost it. It is so easy to take things for granted and I am no different from others. Now I can say from the bottom of my heart that life is sacred. When I hear of life being abused and life being destroyed so easily as it is in my own country, I know of pain within my very being. While death on the streets of Northern Ireland is broadcast almost daily on our news bulletins, I feel a deep sadness that it is often reported as another statistic. Churchmen, politicians, community workers are stretched to find new words to describe acts of terrorism and destruction. And when people are killed by mistake and empty apologetic words are being expressed, my guts turn over as I try to hold in my mind and in my heart the saddened relatives. I can hardly remember what it was like to have one full day of real health and the loss is severe. I groan inwardly when I hear of life itself being shattered or destroyed. Life is sacred, health is sacred, people are sacred. I remember reading in a newspaper last year of a young policeman who was shot in the back in an English town. Apparently he had tried to foil a bank robbery. This had nothing to do with the vicious circle of hatred and bitterness being experienced in Northern Ireland. It was something that could happen in any town or city in the world. Anyway, the bullet had destroyed his spine and he ended up in a wheelchair. He received a special award for bravery. A number of months later, it was reported in the newspapers that he had taken his own life and some reporters wrote about the loneliness and isolation which he had felt and how his sense of loss simply overwhelmed him. When I read the story, I felt as if I knew him and I quietly said a prayer for him and his family.

Battles may occur in any part of the world as people demand their rights and I do believe in civil rights for all. But a right which is demanded without a realisation that it carries an equally important duty or responsibility is almost a misuse of the word. That these things happen is as much a reflection of the broken spirit of man as it is a recognition of man's basic rights. But how can one demand civil rights when one annihilates the basic right of every human being — the right to life?

I do not want this to be a political message and when I sat with these thoughts in prayer, I came up with my own prayer —

> Father,
> All-powerful, give us strength in our weakness,
> Heal the bitter wounds of our society,
> Be our guide and leader
>   in every difficult situation.
> Lord Jesus,
> Our Way, our Truth and our Life,
> Direct our way forward in your steps,
> Keep our hearts fixed on what is true and noble,
> Nourish us with your life in the face of fear and
>   death.
> Holy Spirit,
> Comforter of the weak and distressed,
> Fill our homes with your presence,
> Restore to our hearts your peace and consolation,
> Remove anxiety and distress from our minds.
> Mary,
> Queen of earth and Mother of God,
> Enwrap with your mantle of love the
>   lonely and unloved,
> Teach us the meaning of suffering and pain,
> Help us to stay close to your Son,
> That the darkness of this age may not
>   overwhelm us,
> But that everywhere and at all times,
> All that we do and suffer may be a
>   share in your Son's
> Suffering and death.

Restore to our broken community,
Health in mind and body,
That the peace of Christ may be felt
   in our hearts,
Our homes, our parish and our world,
Now and for ever.
Amen.

Yes, I am a Catholic priest and I still want to respond to whatever that may mean. One of the greatest gifts which I have received, and I believe the sickness of multiple sclerosis was a major factor in it, is the deep faith I have in the living and loving God. Obviously my image of God has been changed or rather developed over the years. The anger which I felt and still feel at times against God, rather than causing me to reject him, has only made him more real. Thankfully, even in the midst of my angry outbursts at the Divinity, I am also able to sit, relax and just know of his tenderness and kindness.

At my death, the only thing that will really matter for me, is how God and I relate. So I can honestly and genuinely thank him for the gift of awareness of his ever-presence. I am also aware of how I fail in that relationship so often — I regret the times when I allow my anger to smoulder and become resentment. But I know that I am always learning and it's foolish of me to think that I should be able to grasp the full plan of God for me in my life. For some strange Godly reason, this is how he wants me to be his priest. I wish I were a better one. I suppose, as Dr Kubler-Ross may say, I have a lot of unfinished business to which to attend.

The first priest I knew with MS I met in a film. It is an old film now, called *The Cardinal*. In one scene, the young, ambitious, proud priest is sent to a run-down parish to be assistant to an old parish priest... a parish priest who had been a continual failure, failure in the sense that he created a lot of debt in past parishes and he just did not respond to the various demands of his parishes. While there, the young priest had to call the doctor to see the parish priest, as he seemed unwell. After an examination, the doctor announced to the young priest that his pastor had multiple sclerosis. Naturally the young man asked the nature of such an illness, to which the doctor replied, 'It is a sickness whereby a person begins to die very slowly from his mid-thirties.' It had been one year since my own diagnosis and my stomach almost turned as I viewed this film.

Already I can hear people say, 'But sure, everyone is dying slowly from the mid-thirties,' and that is true. The big difference is that the person with MS knows of that every day in a real and physical way in his or her body.

The old parish priest in the film was depicted as a holy and humble man, a man alive with the God whom he loved. I suppose that is the challenge facing every Christian and not just the priest. Maybe my MS will enable me to get in touch with my own unfinished business, will make me more aware of my weaknesses and failings, may create space for me to work more intensively with my relationship with God. I still think I resemble more the ambitious, proud young priest — but life is good, people are good and I pray for the openness which I need in order to be God's worker and friend.

I suppose my biggest fear is the unknown of the future. Will I ever be able to say with full conviction, 'I accept myself as I am, MS and all'? Will it always remain benign? If, and God forbid, my MS progresses in any way, will I have to begin again working through a new series of denial, depression, bargaining and so on, especially when I am so fully aware of the fact that I am still trying to say '*Adsum*'? I won't ever be really free of the tension, the battle, the stress of coping with MS, just as no-one is free of the battle of life. Death, it is said, is the great healer and that is true — but like most of my fellow travellers on life's road, I don't want to die just yet. Nor do I want to be limited beyond what limits MS has put on me and continues to put on me. And it may be that only on my death-bed will I be able to say with true conviction, '*Adsum*'.

This book may be finished and yet in a truer sense, it is in itself but a chapter in my life. I don't know what is round the corner and with everyone else I share that same fear. My own acceptance of MS is not yet complete because my life is not yet complete. I want to live as fully as I can.... I want to be a priest.... I want to be happy.... I don't want to be a burden.... I want to give of myself... and I want to be me... and I wonder... and will probably go on wondering.... I have not got all the answers.... I haven't even got all the questions.... My personal struggle with life and sickness mingled with my faith in God has helped to crystallise a little better my own relationship with God.... Yes, I still cry, I still wonder why... and because I ask so much and question so much, I spend more time with my God and I know that has helped.... And maybe it is precisely in the vagueness and darkness of my living that I will be able to respond to a God who lies hidden.... And maybe that is how my suffering unites me with Jesus Christ.... I must carry my own darkness, my own limp faith and continue believing... and I share this with every human being who knows what it is to be human.